CREATIVE
HOMEOWNER®

DESIGN IDEAS for
Baby Rooms

CREATIVE HOMEOWNER®, Upper Saddle River, New Jersey

COPYRIGHT © 2009

CRE▲TIVE
HOMEOWNER®

A Division of Federal Marketing Corp.
Upper Saddle River, NJ

DESIGN IDEAS FOR BABY ROOMS

SENIOR EDITOR	Kathie Robitz
EDITOR	Lisa Kahn
CONTRIBUTING EDITOR	Susan Hillstrom
SENIOR GRAPHIC DESIGN COORDINATOR	Glee Barre
PHOTO COORDINATORS	Robyn Poplasky, Mary Dolan
JUNIOR EDITOR	Jennifer Calvert
DIGITAL IMAGING SPECIALIST	Frank Dyer
INDEXER	Schroeder Indexing Services
COVER DESIGN	Glee Barre
FRONT COVER PHOTOGRAPHY	(clockwise from left) courtesy of PoshTots.com; courtesy of Posh Tots.com; courtesy of York Wallcoverings; courtesy of Fawn and Forest; Tony Giammarino/Giammarino & Dworkin, design by Karen Adams; courtesy of Land of Nod
BACK COVER PHOTOGRAPHY	(left) Mark Lohman, design by Rugrat Habitats/Little Crown Interiors; (top right) Karyn R. Millet, design by Bonesteel Trout Hall; (bottom right) Mark Lohman, design by Rugrat Habitat/Little Crown Interiors

CREATIVE HOMEOWNER

VICE PRESIDENT AND PUBLISHER	Timothy O. Bakke
MANAGING EDITOR	Fran J. Donegan
ART DIRECTOR	David Geer
PRODUCTION COORDINATOR	Sara M. Markowitz

Current Printing (last digit)
10 9 8 7 6 5 4 3 2 1

Design Ideas for Baby Rooms
Library of Congress Control Number: 2008921445
ISBN-10: 1-58011-214-5
ISBN-13: 978-1-58011-214-7

Manufactured in the United States of America

CREATIVE HOMEOWNER®
A Division of Federal Marketing Corp.
24 Park Way
Upper Saddle River, NJ 07458
www.creativehomeowner.com

Planet Friendly Publishing
- ✔ Made in the United States
- ✔ Printed on Recycled Paper

Text: 10%   Cover: 10%
Learn more: www.greenedition.org

GREEN EDITION

At Creative Homeowner we're committed to producing books in an earth-friendly manner and to helping our customers make greener choices.

Manufacturing books in the United States ensures compliance with strict environmental laws and eliminates the need for international freight shipping, a major contributor to global air pollution.

And printing on recycled paper helps minimize our consumption of trees, water, and fossil fuels. *Design Ideas for Baby Rooms* was printed on paper made with 10% post-consumer waste. According to Environmental Defense's Paper Calculator, by using this innovative paper instead of conventional papers, we achieved the following environmental benefits:

Trees Saved: 26

Water Saved: 9,642 gallons

Solid Waste Eliminated: 1,595 pounds

Air Emissions Eliminated: 2,941 pounds

For more information on our environmental practices, please visit us online at www.creativehomeowner.com/green

Acknowledgments

Many thanks to those who gave their generous support in the development of this book, including Little Crown Interiors/Rugrat Habitats, Leslie Saul & Associates, Posh Tots, Boodalee, and York Wallcoverings.

Contents

A s soon as many parents discover that they're expecting a baby, they begin to think about the beautiful nursery they will create to welcome their newborn. Depending upon their particular taste and imagination, this dream room may be a pastel-color cocoon loaded with cushy bedding, delicate curtains, and cuddly stuffed toys. Or it might be a faithful re-creation of a favorite hobby, sport, or literary character. Unfortunately, there's something wrong with both of these

Introduction

pictures—first, indulging in them could put you way over budget, and second, some of these fantasy items are actually not good for baby.

Design Ideas for Baby Rooms is a source for the latest in design and childproofing tips to help you create a nursery that is stylish, soothing, and safe. And because the peacefully sleeping infant in the nursery today will be an active tot before you know it, there is also a chapter with ideas for toddler rooms that takes a peek into the future to help you plan ahead.

Hopefully, this book will inspire you to make smart decisions now that can save you money, time, and energy as you adapt your new baby's space to his ever-growing requirements.

LEFT A chenille-covered armchair tucked into a corner creates a cozy haven for late-night feedings.

ABOVE In this modern nursery, vibrant color on the walls and accessories adds punch to the simple white crib and chest.

BELOW This dreamy baby's room features a vintage-style storage chest with sweet, handpainted details.

1

Make Room for Baby

Preparing for the arrival of a new family member is a very special time, and one of its most satisfying elements can be getting the nursery ready. It's tempting to express your joy by purchasing every piece of furniture and equipment you can find. But if you're not careful, what should be a peaceful space can become cluttered. Before you are overwhelmed with nesting urges, take the time to plan a design that makes sense for you and your new baby.

- begin with the basics
- finding the space
- do you need a pro?
- a small investment

The ideal baby's room is both pretty and practical. This blue-and-white space is also peaceful, another essential quality.

begin with the basics

before you choose a single paint swatch, familiarize yourself with some fundamental design principles. You probably already know what you like, and you may have successfully combined furniture, fabrics, and colors in other rooms in your home. However, baby's room is different. Once the nesting instinct kicks in, many parents go a little crazy, perhaps even trying to re-create their own childhood fantasies of the perfect nursery. You can keep potential decorating excesses in check by focusing on the time-honored principles of scale, proportion, line, balance, harmony, and rhythm.

Scale and **proportion** are similar terms. Scale refers to the size of an object compared with the size of everything else in the room. Proportion refers to the relationship of objects to one another based on their size. Proper scale is achieved when all of the elements of a design scheme are in correct proportion, not only to one another but also to the whole room. The principles of scale and proportion pertain to all of the features in a room, from windows and doors to furniture, accessories, window treatments, and even patterns, prints, and color. All of these objects should be scaled to the size of the room and proportional to the other items in the room.

You can create scale and proportion in the baby's room by paying attention to the items you choose. For example, a large chest of drawers might overwhelm a small bedroom meant for a baby. Conversely, a child-size bureau or delicate feeding chair will look out of proportion with an adult-height changing table.

OPPOSITE, ABOVE, AND RIGHT Rejecting traditional nursery furniture—much of which tends to be too sweet and fussy—many young parents are now choosing contemporary, sophisticated pieces that blend with the rest of their home's decor. The handsome crib shown here will grow with the child, easily converting to a toddler bed. The rest of the clean-lined, gender-neutral pieces will be useful from toddlerhood through high school and will mesh with virtually any design scheme. In a fundamentally neutral room such as this one, a patterned area rug (opposite and inset, right) could provide a bright spot of color.

the principle of line

OPPOSITE Vertical lines on the wall create the illusion of height in this toddler's room. A handpainted chest, mosaic tile mirror, and vintage ballet portraits lend delicate charm.

BELOW RIGHT An old stepladder strikes a lively note and doubles as a unique display for toys. A bold mural painted on the wall also enlivens the room.

Designers often describe a space in terms of its lines. For example, vertical lines, in the form of columns, high ceilings, or tall windows, add height to a room; they will also offset the predominantly horizontal lines of most furniture. Horizontal lines imply security and relaxation, while diagonals suggest motion and movement or lead the eye to a desired place. The curved lines of an arched window, an oval table, or an overstuffed armchair create an aura of freedom, softness, and sensuality.

Keeping in mind the principles of scale and proportion, try to incorporate a variety of lines into baby's room. Create interest by throwing in some curves or diagonals with furniture, moldings, or accessories. In a small room, add width with horizontally striped wallcovering; add height with vertical stripes or a tall piece of furniture.

head start

Invest wisely in items, such as wallpaper, furniture, and window treatments, that aren't overly babyish. Soon enough, your newborn will be a toddler who will likely want a room that declares he's a "big kid."

rhythm and harmony

With harmony, elements work together to produce cohesiveness. It's not necessary that colors and patterns match exactly—that would be boring—but that they relate closely or contrast subtly. As harmony pulls a room together, rhythm moves the eye around, following colors, textures, and shapes to bring the space to life. Like the other design principles, harmony and rhythm create a visually pleasing interior scene. "When your eye moves peacefully across a space you experience visual serenity," says interior designer Patricia Gaylor.

"Too many colors or colors that contrast too sharply can be disruptive to the eye. Even an ultralarge piece of furniture that knocks the whole room out of scale is enough to disrupt a harmonious scene."

To achieve balance in your design, pay attention to the placement of objects according to their visual weight, says Gaylor. When the balance is right, relationships between the objects will seem natural and comfortable to the eye, resulting in visual equilibrium, a soothing and desirable state for a room where baby will be spending those first few months of life. For example, two framed pictures hanging side by side will please the eye if they are roughly the same size and weight; but two pictures of unequal size will disturb the eye. However, not all balance must be symmetrical; asymmetrical balance often creates pleasing and interesting effects—provided the scale is correct. One example might be a grouping of tall, slender objects on one side of a mantelpiece and a short, wide vase on the other.

a well-balanced nursery evokes a peaceful feeling

To create harmony in this room, the designer focused on a couple of colors and combined them effectively. The asymmetrical letters above the crib provide rhythm and interest.

OPPOSITE The skillful use of wallcovering patterns and coordinating borders can jazz up a room and make it look larger, both vertically and horizontally.

BELOW Placed on the diagonal, this crib creates the illusion of greater width in a narrow room. The washable wallpaper features leaping frogs for baby's amusement.

bare-bones budget?

If need be, you can furnish baby's room frugally with second-hand furniture, then spruce it up with fresh paint. Also be on the lookout for garage-sale toys and accessories, and blankets, pillows, and crib bumpers handed down from close friends or relatives.

visual tricks

Aside from doing major structural work, how do you deal with an oddly-shaped room? Designers have developed some clever ways to disguise or draw attention away from such jarring imperfections.

Long. If the nursery is long, divide the space by creating two or more furniture groupings. For example, use the crib as the focal point for the sleeping area; then put a dresser, rocking chair, table, and lamp in another part of the room.

Narrow. You can make a narrow space look wider by placing furniture on the diagonal. Place the crib cater-cornered and introduce as many squares into the room as possible. One example would be to group art in a square arrangement on the wall; use a cube-shaped dresser or chest; and hang a large square mirror on a major wall.

Too low. A room with a low ceiling can feel cramped and closed-in. In general, use as many vertical lines as possible to add height and eliminate the claustrophobic feeling. Adding an armoire or tall, narrow bookcases, for example, will create a sense of expansiveness. Hanging floor-length curtains above the window frame at ceiling level can also create the illusion of height. Vertically striped curtain fabrics or wallcoverings are other good options for a low-ceiling room.

Too tall. If the ceiling is too high, the scale of the space can be lowered by incorporating more horizontal lines in the room. For instance, walls will appear shorter if molding is installed halfway or three-quarters of the way up. Also, hang pictures lower on the wall.

Too angular. Some rooms—such as those built under attic eaves—may seem "chopped up" because they contain too many angles. To unify such a space, choose one color or pattern for all the surfaces, including the ceiling. Alternatively, you can play up interesting angles by giving each surface a different treatment.

RIGHT You don't need a lot of space for nursery basics. Even an alcove in a larger room will do in a pinch.

OPPOSITE In this house, an older-child's room was partitioned to make room for baby.

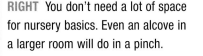ow that you understand several tried-and-true principles for creating a harmonious design, the next question is where the baby's room will be located. If this is your first child and you're lucky enough to own a house with several bedrooms—or at least one extra room—you'll have little problem finding a space to designate as the nursery. But if all of your bedrooms are occupied and space is tight, you may need to get creative. Perhaps you can carve out space in an existing room that doesn't get much use, such as a guest room, sewing room, or even a home office. With careful planning you'll probably be able to fit in all of the equipment the baby needs. You might also consider making space for the nursery in your own bedroom or in an older child's room. Another solution: convert existing, unused space into a room. Is there a dead-end hall in your house? There may be enough room in it for baby-room basics. How about an extra-large closet or two good-size closets that share a wall? A situation such as this could easily lend itself to a new room with only a minimum of construction. Perhaps your house has an extra-roomy bedroom that can be divided into two smaller ones. If so, all you need to do is put

finding the space

up a new wall, prep it, paint it, and add some architectural trim. It will look like it's always been there. Also, take a look at the attic. Is it in good enough shape—and accessible enough—to become a nursery? Converting an attic into a nursery is more complex than just dividing a big room in half because you will probably need to add heating, cooling, and ventilating systems and upgrade electrical wiring. Still, it may be worth it. With a baby monitor and a staircase that's easy to negotiate, you can respond to a crying baby in a flash—and you've solved your space problem.

get web savvy

Check out baby-furniture companies on the Internet. Some of them offer free nursery-planning guides complete with graph paper, furniture cutouts, and helpful hints.

location, location

If possible, position baby's room near a bathroom and away from street noise and the hubbub of household activity.

OPPOSITE
This luxurious nursery suite has got it all—an easy chair for nighttime feedings, a window seat, a soft rug to cushion falls, and a deep drawer for toy storage.

RIGHT An adjoining bathroom, painted the same soothing green, is another of the luxuries offered by the opulent baby suite.

sweet dreams

RIGHT Perched under the eaves, a remodeled attic becomes a perfect bedroom for twins.

BELOW AND OPPOSITE The simple room below is suitable for a toddler and his older brother. A blue-and-white room shared by a baby and her older sister is appropriately feminine but not babyish, thus ensuring the occupants will grow into it.

create a cozy space for baby and sibling to share

sharing space

If baby must share a room with an older sibling, pare down nursery furniture to the minimum and set up your nursing chair in another room where late-night feedings won't wake your other child.

law and order

Be sure to acquire permits from your local building authority for any major remodeling or new construction you are planning. In most towns, failure to do so could result in penalties and hefty fines.

i f you need to alter your living space to make room for baby, you may need professional assistance. On the other hand, skilled do-it-yourself enthusiasts with a good amount of experience can probably handle the work themselves. (See "Who Should do the Work?" on page 28 to assess your own abilities.)

If you're going to hire a professional, chose one who's right for the job. To build an addition or make significant alterations to interior space, you will almost certainly need a general contractor and possibly an architect or space planner.

do you need a pro?

You can also hire an architect to design the addition for you and oversee the project through its completion. Alternatively, you can employ the architect for design services only, then work with a contractor of your choice. Some municipalities require an architect's plan—whatever the scope of the job—before they will authorize any new construction.

Converting interior space from one use to another is relatively simple and can be done by you, a contractor, or a talented carpenter or general handyman. If your interior remodeling project involves plumbing, heating, or electricity, you'll also need to hire a professional in those trades. For example, if you plan to convert attic space to a nursery, you may want to add a bath at the same time so that the room can eventually be used for an older child or an overnight guest. In this case, you would need professionals to install the required systems.

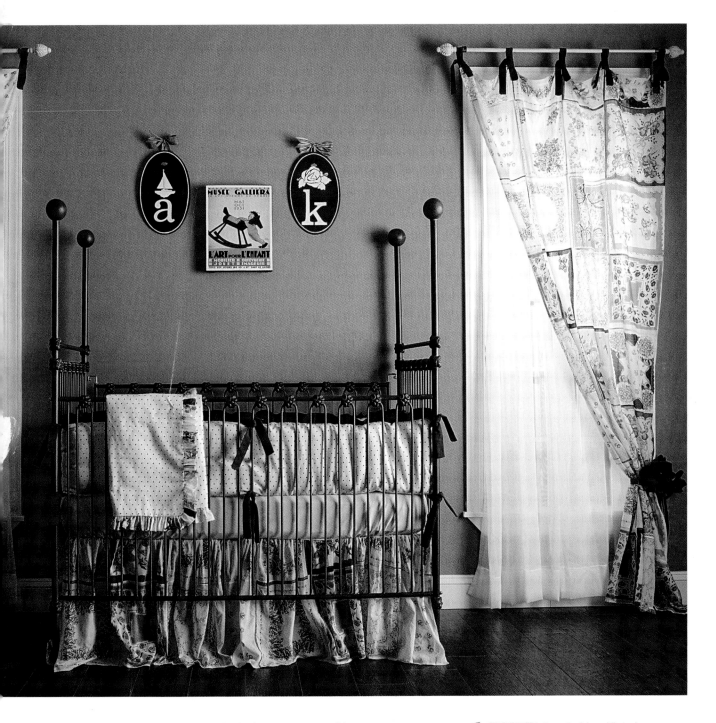

Once you've created a space for baby, you can call in an interior designer to help you decorate—or hire someone to help you create it from scratch. Anyone with a degree in interior design has been trained in space planning, construction (including creating working drawings and specifications), ergonomics, lighting, and surface treatments such as furnishings, paint, fabrics, wallcoverings, and accessories. Because they have access to showrooms, interior designers can also expand the decorative possibilities and choices for your baby's room.

OPPOSITE Located in a Victorian-era house, this former library was converted to a toddler's bedroom by the do-it-your-self owners, using fresh paint, new wall-covering, and elbow grease.

ABOVE Too busy to decorate? An interior designer can help you blend flooring, fabrics, colors, and accessories into a pleasing nursery design.

what the home improvement pros do

- **Architects** plan, design, and oversee new construction and major remodels. You will need one if your new nursery involves an addition or an extensive makeover of existing space.
- **Interior designers** can be of great help in the creation of a visually appealing room and the selection of furniture, fabrics, color, and pattern.
- **Space planners** are experts at organizing interior space; some of them specialize in planning and building in storage and outfitting closets.
- **General contractors** are skilled in all aspects of the remodeling trade. For complex jobs, they usually work from plans drawn up by another professional; for simple remodeling they can translate your ideas into reality.
- **Carpenters** are the people to call if you are simply adding some shelves or cabinets to make baby's room more efficient. A skilled carpenter may also be able to handle simple remodeling projects.

OPPOSITE Raspberry sherbet-color walls lend contemporary pizzazz to baby pink bedding and accessories.

ABOVE Pretty fabrics give even a business-like diapering station a bit of charm.

RIGHT In this freshly wallpapered nursery, tiny white footprints stand out against a cool blue background.

BELOW Contemporary wallcoverings offer a fresh take on standard nursery motifs.

do your homework

Don't restrict your search for a reliable professional to the local phonebook. A splashy ad may indicate that an architect or designer has some money to spend, but it is no guarantee of professionalism, skill, or experience. Membership in trade or professional associations may indicate that a person has met certain industry standards, and these associations are handy for steering you toward likely candidates in your area. But the best route to a reliable professional is through the recommendations of friends, relatives, or other acquaintances that have recently undergone a project similar to the job you are planning. Look carefully at the finished job and ask the right questions: was the contractor easy to work with? Did they show up on time? Adhere to the schedule? Finish the job?

who should do the work?

Is it realistic for you to do all the work yourself? Or should you hire a professional contractor? Perhaps the answer is some combination of the two. To make an honest evaluation, consider these eight questions.

1. **How big is the project?** If the room requires only cosmetic help to make it baby-ready, even a novice with sufficient interest can pick up the necessary skills. An individual who has some experience with residential makeovers can certainly do a fine job. However, when some special work—such as electrical wiring or painting a mural (right and below) needs to be done, hire a professional.

2. **Do you have enough time to commit to the project?** You can probably paint the walls in a weekend, but think about how much time it will take to shop for, order, and assemble new furniture, or to strip down and repaint vintage pieces. If you're also working outside the home or if you have small children to care for, these time-consuming tasks can get overwhelming pretty quickly.

3. **Do you have the temperament to get the whole project done yourself?** If you are naturally patient and persistent and enjoy creating things, the do-it-yourself route may be perfect for you. However, if you become impatient when the

bolt and nut doesn't easily fit where the directions say they should or the chair rail isn't plumb, you won't fully enjoy what should be a delightful experience. If you tend to get frustrated by snags, ask for—or hire—help. Don't start something you won't be able to finish.

4. **Do you enjoy—and are you able to do—physical work?** If you have some experience with removing and hanging wallpaper, installing flooring material, or refinishing furniture, you know what tasks you can do and which you enjoy (or don't). If these are new to you and your design plan calls for such skills, it may be a good idea to enlist the help of a friend who has been through the paces. With the materials, tools, and instructional help available today, don't automatically rule out doing it without professional help. You can probably pick up the know-how quickly with a little hands-on guidance from an experienced do-it-yourselfer or by attending a workshop at a home center.

5. **Have you ever done any of this kind of work before?** Even if you are a complete novice, it's not impossible for you to accomplish wonders, but you have to ask yourself how much you want to struggle. (See questions 1 and 4.)

6. Do you have the tools you'll need to do specific jobs?
Hanging wallpaper, installing window shades—even painting
stripes—all require tools. If you don't already have them, can
you borrow them? If you'll need to purchase them, consider
whether it would be less expensive to hire a professional.

7. Can you get help if you need it? Sometimes a task requires
more than two hands. Will someone be available to lend a
hand or two when you need it? Also, do you have a knowl-
edgeable source to call if you have questions or run into
problems you can't handle yourself?

**8. Does your plan and budget have enough "wiggle room"
to be adjusted in case you discover you can't do it yourself?** If you hit a snag you can't handle, would you consider
changing the plan? Or if you make a mistake you can't fix
without assistance, are you be prepared to call in someone
to help you? Both situations may affect your budget.

a small investment

p utting together a nursery is relatively inexpensive compared to remodeling a bath or kitchen. You may already have a room designated for baby, and if this child isn't your first, you may have most of the furniture you need waiting in the garage or basement. But if new construction is necessary to create a nursery, you'll need to consider professional fees. Even diehard do-it-yourselfers agree that seeking professional help is sometimes the most cost-effective way to get a job accomplished.

Interior designers can actually save you money. For example, their expertise allows them to re-imagine your space and your belongings and reuse many of the things you already own. These professionals can also provide tips on eliminating clutter, using color effectively, and coordinating prints and fabrics. Many of them will work on an hourly basis, particularly for a small space, and consultation fees can begin at around $100 dollars per hour. You may also pick up free design advice where you shop for baby furniture or nursery accessories.

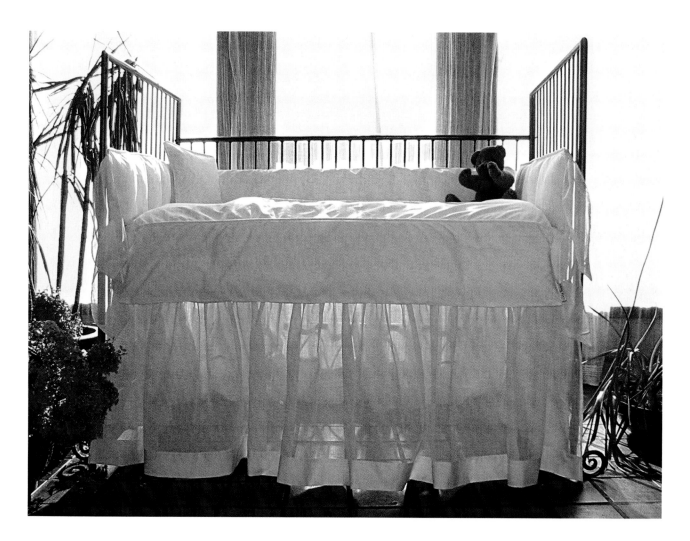

OPPOSITE Provided they meet safety recommendations, vintage cribs make charming additions to baby rooms.

LEFT A hutch, useful and flexible, can hold toys now, books, and media equipment later.

BELOW When baby becomes a toddler, this built-in diaper-changing station can serve as a bureau.

adding it up

To determine how much to budget for the services of a contractor, carpenter, painter, electrician, or handyman, get two or three estimates. Most contractors will gladly provide one, and their review of what your job entails will be educational for you.

Whatever the final figure is on the estimate, pad it a little. A 20-percent comfort zone isn't unreasonable. First, you will be prepared for problems that neither you nor your contractor can foresee. Second, the padding will cover unexpected "better-way costs." When, in the middle of a job, the contractor says, "I can do it the way we discussed for the price we established, or I can do it another, better way that will cost a little more," that padding can come in mighty handy.

2

Color and Pattern

One of the most delightful tasks in setting up baby's room—and later transforming it into a special space for a toddler—is choosing the colors and patterns. Of course, you can always opt for the traditional pink for girls and blue for boys. But you also have the opportunity to do something creative and unique. By the time your child is a toddler, she will likely have her own opinions. And while it's impossible to predict what her tastes will be, you can lay the foundation now for a room that will grow beautifully with your child.

- **developing a color scheme**
- **color through baby's eyes**
- **the power of color and pattern**
- **mix and match**
- **rooms with a theme**

Cloyingly cute baby rooms are a thing of the past—today's designs are smart and sophisticated.

do you lack the confidence to pick a color for your baby's room? Don't lose heart and paint everything white. Instead, develop your innate sense of color harmony and get creative. Here's some background information to get you started.

You can arrive at a color scheme by trial and error, or you can be a bit more scientific by using the color wheel as a guide. (See page 39.) To use the color wheel, begin by selecting a basic color that appeals to you; then use the wheel to choose additional hues to form your color scheme. There are several types of color schemes.

developing a color scheme

A **monochromatic** scheme is based on one color, such as all blue or all green. Sound dull? It won't be if you use different intensities of a single color, such as navy blue paired with light denim, or lime with kelly green. You can mix up a monochromatic scheme even more by including a variety of patterns and textures in the same colorway. Add extra spice by introducing accent colors in bed linens, curtains, rugs, pillows, and accessories.

To create an **analogous** scheme, choose colors that are next to one another on the color wheel. Examples are pink, which is red tinted with white, paired with nearby purple (red-violet). Again, you can play with color intensity, textures, and patterns to add interest.

Selecting two colors that are opposite each other on the color wheel—such as blue and orange—results in a **complementary** scheme. These colors blend warmth and coolness for a lively visual effect. And while combining two complementary colors at their full intensity might be jarring—and too bright for a baby's room—here is where tinting comes in handy. By mixing bright blue with white, it becomes a soft, powdery blue; white added to orange transforms it into a peaceful peach.

If you use three or more colors that are equidistant on the color wheel you create a **triadic** scheme. A combination of red, yellow, and blue is one example; a palette of lighter tints—pink, pale yellow, and powder blue—is another.

Hopefully this information will demystify the process of developing a color scheme and help you create harmony in the nursery. Spend a little time studying the wheel. Then get in touch with your artistic side, and trust yourself to select the colors that suit you perfectly.

LEFT As this cozy corner proves, design success is practically guaranteed if you follow the principles of scale and proportion and select complementary colors for walls, window treatments, and accessories.

OPPOSITE Filled with furniture, fabrics, and toys, this nursery could have become a jumbled mess. Luckily, the skillful use of color has given it balance and order.

light and color

Because artificial and natural light dramatically affect the way color looks in any given space, those little color chips you get in paint stores or home centers may not look the same once they are painted on the walls of your baby's room.

For example, if the room faces north, the natural light will be bluer and cooler, intensifying cool colors and cooling down warmer hues. On the other hand, rooms with southern exposures will be filled for most of the day with warm, yellow-toned light. East-facing rooms are sunny in the morning; west-facing windows receive late-afternoon sun.

To get an accurate reading of the way light influences your color choices, do an on-site test. Paint a large swath on the wall and study it several times a day as the light moves through the room. Based on these observations, you may decide to adjust the color, choose a different one, or use window treatments and artificial lighting to create the hues and intensities that you want.

ABOVE Adding color to the nursery with toys and accessories helps baby to develop his visual sense.

RIGHT Abundant sun streams through the windows of this toddler's room, washing the yellow-gold walls with light and making the color pop. Ivory floors, woodwork, and furniture reflect the light to further brighten the room.

RIGHT Babies love silly, whimsical wall art in their rooms—and the more colorful it is, the better. This wall appliqué helps teach a toddler the alphabet and the names of animals.

BELOW Here, trucks of all kinds decorate the walls and the fronts of the handy storage bins under this toddler's bed. The rug, bed linens, and beanbag chair take color cues from the wallcovering.

a little color sense goes a long way

color vocabulary

The following terms are used to identify types of colors or explain their interrelationships.

- **Advancing colors:** Warm colors and dark colors, which seem to advance toward you.
- **Analogous colors:** Any three colors located next to one another on the color wheel.
- **Color scheme:** A group of colors used together to create visual harmony.
- **Color wheel:** A circular arrangement of the twelve basic colors that shows how they relate to one another.
- **Complementary colors:** Colors located opposite one another on the color wheel.
- **Contrast:** Using colors with different values and intensities in different proportions to create visual harmony in a color scheme.
- **Cool colors:** Greens, blues, and violets.
- **Double-split complementary colors:** The colors located on each side of two complementary colors on the color wheel.
- **Earth tones:** The neutral colors that dominate in nature.
- **Hue:** Synonym for color. Used most often to describe the family to which a color belongs.
- **Intensity:** The brightness or dullness of a color. Also referred to as a color's purity or saturation.
- **Intermediate colors:** Red-orange, yellow-orange, yellow-green, blue-green, blue-violet, and red-violet; the six colors made by mixing equal amounts of a primary and secondary color.
- **Native colors:** The basic inorganic pigments derived from minerals, used to make the colors found in artist's oil paints.
- **Pastel:** A color to which a lot of white has been added to make it very light in value.
- **Primary colors:** Red, yellow, and blue; the three colors in the visible spectrum that cannot be broken down into other colors. In various combinations and proportions, they make all other colors.
- **Quaternary colors:** Colors made by mixing two tertiary colors.
- **Receding colors:** Cool colors and light colors, which make surfaces seem farther from the eye.
- **Secondary colors:** Orange, green, and violet; the colors made by mixing equal amounts of two primary colors.
- **Shade:** A color to which black has been added to make it darker.
- **Split complementary:** A color paired with the colors on each side of its complementary color.
- **Tertiary colors:** Colors made by combining two secondary colors.
- **Tint:** A color to which white has been added to make it lighter in value.
- **Tone:** A color to which gray has been added to change its value.
- **Triad:** Any three colors located equidistant from one another on the color wheel.
- **Value:** The lightness (tint or pastel) and darkness (shade) of a color.
- **Value scale:** A graphic tool used to show the range of values between pure white and true black.
- **Warm colors**: Reds, oranges, yellows, and browns.

color through baby's eyes

a s you think about color possibilities for the nursery, be aware that color can affect one's perception of a space, including how large or small it seems. You don't need a science degree to use color to its best advantage, just a few pointers. For example, if the baby's room is large, you can make it cozy by selecting warmer, deeper colors. If the room is small, cool or pale colors may make it appear more spacious.

Don't let the retreating nature of cool colors fool you. In its lightest tints, or mixed with a touch of gray, blue is calming as well as space enhancing. But if you're determined to use bright blue, make sure it's crisp and fresh with plenty of white trim and accents.

BELOW Hang soft, colorful toys—such as these tied to the handle of an infant carrier—where the baby can see them and follow their movement.

OPPOSITE According to recent scientific studies, color and pattern in the nursery stimulate baby and enhance brain development.

warm it up

The warm colors of the spectrum are lively and stimulating. Reds are festive, yellows feel cheery, and orange is earthy. They all energize the ambiance of a room.

Although babies don't notice color in their first few months of life, some experts believe that an ultrabright, hot color on the nursery walls will eventually have an adverse affect, overstimulating baby and making him restless. Don't give up on warm colors altogether; instead, consider using a tint of a special favorite. Red can be lightened to ribbon pink or strawberry. With the addition of white, traffic-sign yellow becomes buttermilk, soft lemon, or a yellow so creamy it almost qualifies as neutral. Flaming orange? Too brash; but pale peach or delicate orange blossom would be lovely in a nursery.

Earth tones, such as terra-cotta, burnt orange, and olive green, are warm colors in a subdued form. Too rich for a baby's room, perhaps, but warm and inviting when relaxed into shades such as honey, mocha, and pale celadon.

BELOW Serene yet warm, pale lemon yellow is a popular nursery color.

OPPOSITE TOP Gender-specific colors may be passé for some, but pink is still a favorite for many a little girl's room.

OPPOSITE BOTTOM A splash of yellow, such as in this upholstered chair, adds warm color to the nursery without being overwhelming.

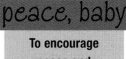

peace, baby

To encourage peace and tranquility in the nursery, use a soft shade of pink, coral, or peach on the ceiling, an area that baby gazes at often throughout the day.

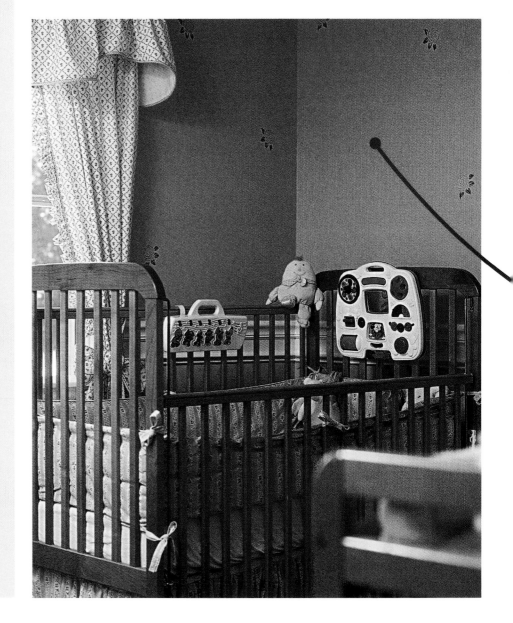

mellow yellow

There is evidence that a nursery painted bright yellow causes an infant to cry more. Try a softer buttercream or pale lemon instead.

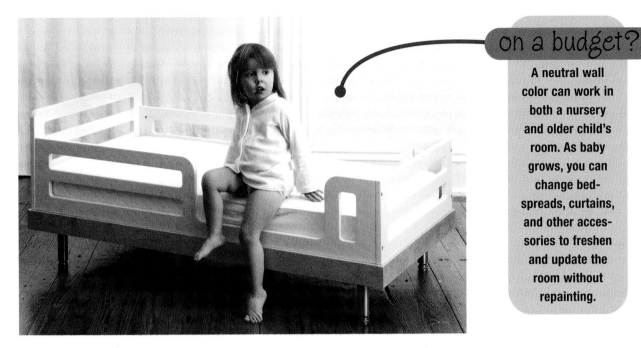

on a budget?

A neutral wall color can work in both a nursery and older child's room. As baby grows, you can change bed-spreads, curtains, and other acces-sories to freshen and update the room without repainting.

nifty neutrals

Sometimes dismissed as too bland, neutral colors encompass a huge array of tones from cool to warm, many of them quite interesting and appealing. Strictly speaking, they range from white to black and include all the grays, but off-white, creams, and soft shades of brown, such as taupe, khaki, tan, and ecru, are also consid-ered neutrals, as are certain very pale shades of other colors.

Neutrals effectively enhance the visual flow of space and can make a small nursery feel more expansive. They also provide a low-key backdrop for showcas-ing vividly colored toys, artwork, and other items.

OPPOSITE TOP Graduating to a toddler's bed is an important childhood event. This bed, painted a neutral, creamy white, will blend with any decorating scheme you and your toddler choose.

BELOW An all-white color scheme creates a light, airy ambiance. If at any point you decide you want color you can always introduce it through curtains, rugs, or bed linens.

RIGHT Whimsical hand-painted murals stand out dramatically against a neutral backdrop. In the elegant vintage cradle, parents can rock the baby gently to sleep.

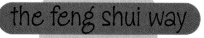

the feng shui way

The Asian philosophy of feng shui suggests that white is the best baby-room color because it is associated with creativity; a soft muted color, they say, will promote rest and health.

in the pink

To keep pale-pink nursery walls from looking bland—or bright pink from looking like bubblegum—temper the color with white paint on furniture and woodwork.

baby's room should be restful, but not boring

create contrast

Yes, you want baby's first room to be calming and soothing, but you don't want it to look bland and boring. Fortunately, adding some contrast will banish any possibility of the blahs. For instance, pairing a neutral hue with pure-white trim will brighten it and bring out its warmth. Likewise, combining shades, such as a deep beige on the walls with a paler tint on the ceiling and woodwork, can create surprising richness.

But beware of too much contrast, which can create an awkward, unbalanced look. If, for example, you have inherited some baby furniture in dark, heavy-looking wood—or found it at a lawn sale—don't paint the nursery walls white or a very light color. In this scenario, the contrast would make the furniture stand out awkwardly. Instead, paint the walls a slightly darker hue or wallpaper them in a small-scale pattern with a little contrast. Another idea: paint the furniture white or creamy-white for a lighter look all around. (See Chapter 7 for guidelines on nontoxic paints.)

ABOVE In this baby's room, white paint works wonders, sprucing up a couple of pieces of flea-market furniture and providing contrast to the light pink walls.

RIGHT Decorating principles at work— a checkerboard theme and the selection of harmonious colors beautify this little nursery. White curtains and crib pull it all together.

Conventional wisdom states that babies are not able to perceive color until they are two or three months old; until then, they see mostly black and white and, possibly, red. Other theories suggest that they do see colors but cannot distinguish them clearly until they are a few months older. We do know that black-and-white patterns, which offer 100-percent contrast, are the easiest for young infants to see. Studies indicate that in their first month of life, babies can also discern shades of gray; at two months they are capable of perceiving many subtle shadings.

An important pastime for young children is paying attention to the visual world, and color is a key element. Color affects the emotions and stimulates brain development. Within the first years of life, exposure to color and other stimuli helps develop synapses, which are vital chemical connections across nerve cells in the brain. Research shows that stimulation of all the senses in the early years of development give children a heightened predisposition to learning.

the power of color and pattern

Many parents buy high-contrast black-and-white toys and accessories to help their babies develop visual acuity. However, experts say that the normal visual environment is also stimulating to babies. Therefore, pretty much any color that appeals to you is fine for your baby's first room. Do keep in mind, however, that research seems to indicate that very bright shades used in large doses or a great deal of high contrast might actually be too stimulating in a room where you want baby to rest and fall asleep easily. Encourage baby's development with brightly colored pictures, toys, and books instead.

OPPOSITE A striking contemporary print makes an interesting contrast to the vintage-style crib.

BELOW LEFT The bright colors and different textures in this play mat help baby develop all her senses.

BELOW RIGHT These days, many parents prefer a sophisticated look to a traditional, babyish one.

ABOVE Vintage ceramic serving pieces add color and personality while holding baby's supplies.

LEFT The walls, painted an earthy color, promise serenity while the mural supplies something stimulating for baby to see.

OPPOSITE Faced with a tight budget? Try updating hand-me-down furniture—such as this wicker rocker—for use in the nursery.

color therapy

In a study of secondary-school students, a team of researchers discovered that color plays a role in learning. Shades of pink and light blue are downright soothing; almond and pale yellow, they found, are neutral and nonirritating; and green may encourage creativity. Brights, such as yellow, orange, and red, however, are not good colors for the nursery. Vivid yellow, the studies found, excites the brain and body; orange produces agitation; and red stimulates the appetite. These colors might also keep a baby or very young child awake at night, hardly the effect that new parents are looking for.

color power—use it to soothe or stimulate

mix and match

OPPOSITE Wallcovering collections take the guesswork out of combining color and pattern, making it a snap for do-it-yourself decorators to put together a great-looking room.

ABOVE AND BELOW Wallcovering borders are available in a huge array of sizes and styles. Used alone or in conjunction with larger overall patterns, they can create character and pizzazz.

i t's not only paint that brings color and decorative interest to baby's room; there is also pattern, available in the form of wallcoverings, borders, stencils, or in designs that you can paint on walls yourself. To introduce pattern in smaller doses, you can also make effective use of curtains, bed linens, and rugs.

Wallcovering manufacturers sell an enormous number of patterns of all kinds—stripes, checks, flowers, plus every kind of animal found in nature and some found only in fantasy. Much of it is designed expressly for use in nurseries and children's rooms. For optimal results, keep some general guidelines in mind. For example, to make a small room seem more spacious, use a small-scale pattern with a generous amount of light- or medium-tone color as the ground. Large-scale patterns will seem to advance, moving the walls toward you, so using them in a small nursery could create a sense of claustrophobia.

Some popular wallcovering patterns are very bold, all done up in bright primary colors and featuring large-scale objects, and would be best reserved for a toddler's room. A certain amount of visual interest in a baby's room is considered mentally stimulating and conducive to learning; too much may have the opposite effect. Stick to small-scale patterns for a room intended for an infant, say the experts. There are plenty of patterns that provide a little contrast but will not tend to overstimulate baby. The room where baby sleeps should not be so interesting that it keeps her awake.

By the time your baby reaches toddler age, he or she will enjoy and benefit from the stimulation of bolder patterns. Even then, say some experts, it may be best to restrict the wall your child sees from his bed to a solid, soothing color or a small-scale, tranquil pattern.

Wallpaper borders offer a simple way to add just the right amount of pattern to a room. In most rooms of the house, borders are applied just under the ceiling; in rooms designed for little ones, they're best applied lower down—say, chair-rail height—where babies and toddlers can see and enjoy them.

mixing patterns

Here's a designer's trick for mixing patterns successfully, an endeavor that seems daunting to many homeowners—provide links of scale, motif, and color. The regularity of checked, striped, and geometric patterns—particularly if they are small-scale and low-contrast—make them easy to mix. A small floral can play off a thin ticking stripe, but a big splashy floral may require a bolder stripe to create a pleasing, same-scale mix.

The most effective link is shared colors or a similar level of intensity of color between the prints. Make sure all of your patterns contain at least one hue that is similar, even if it's a background or neutral color.

BELOW A perennially popular and classic pattern has more staying power than a trendy one, such as a cartoon character or action figure. Here, coordinated bed-linens did the design work, uniting the decor with stars of different sizes.

RIGHT There's a lot of pattern in this toddler's room. Had it not been mixed by a masterful hand, it might easily have descended into chaos. What makes it work? All of the patterns are simple, proper scale is maintained, and only two colors—blue and yellow—are used.

mixed with a sure hand, patterns add a lively look

adding pattern

Pattern animates a space. Coordinated designs for walls, bedding, curtains, and accessories are readily available. Or get creative and mix and match yourself. Remember— stick to the same colors, but vary the size of the patterns.

overcome flaws with decorative techniques

If you're stuck with an ultrasmall room to serve as the nursery, create the illusion of space by painting walls, ceiling, and furniture the same light color. To brighten a dark room that faces north or east, use warm, pale colors such as pink or peach, and hang a mirror or two to reflect sunlight. In the unlikely event that the nursery should be too large to feel cozy, make it seem snug with warm, rich tones. Large-patterned wallpaper will have a shrinking effect—just make sure it's not too bold for baby—and a darker shade of paint on the ceiling will visually lower it.

OPPOSITE Curtains that hang above the window and pink-and-white-painted stripes that rise to the ceiling give height to this small room.

ABOVE In the same pink-and-white nursery, a collection of antique pottery—safely out of baby's reach— is an unusual, grown-up touch.

LEFT A peg rack provides a display for adorable infant wear.

a nother way to express your nesting instinct while waiting for the baby to arrive is to create a theme for the little darling's room. This theme can be created strictly by you and can focus on anything you like—nature, animals, fairy-tales, sports, favorite pastimes, favorite places, even people and places that are important in your family's life.

The theme can be expressed in several ways. For example, you might commission one or more murals of your favorite vacation spot near the ocean or a scene from a fairy tale that has special meaning for you. Or, confine the theme to a small mural or a stencil on one wall, or a part of one wall, and carry it through to other areas of the room with decorative objects and accessories.

rooms with a theme

Many wallpaper manufacturers offer themed wallcoverings for baby and toddler rooms, so if you're not feeling artistic—or willing to incur the expense of a muralist— check out this option. You can use wallcovering on one or more walls or restrict the theme to borders accompanied by decorative accents.

But don't go overboard. In a nursery, restraint is crucial. Too much color, pattern, and busyness could be upsetting to an infant. Advance your theme simply, with a stencil, a quilt hung on a wall, a picture, or a mobile. By the time your baby reaches toddler age you can let yourself go a little.

Economy is another reason to restrain yourself. Unless you've got money to burn, it's not practical to choose a theme and reinforce it down to the last detail with sheets, pillow cases, comforters, curtains, lamps, wall hangings, mobiles, and more. This kind of design saturation will be overwhelming and uninteresting to begin with and will become old news in a few months. You could be in such a hurry to get rid of it that you won't get your money's worth.

Thinking about a theme for your child's room? Be sure to proceed with caution. The seashore theme shown here is a good example—it's interesting and colorful but not overwhelming.

Go Green

Bamboo bedding is silky-soft, naturally antibacterial, and made from sustainable, organically grown resources.

from a muralist's point of view

Decorative painter Judy Bereczki, who operates out of Montclair, New Jersey, and Delhi, New York, likes to get a sense of what interests a child—and his parents— before she creates a theme for the room. "I spend time in the room, and perhaps meet the child," she says, "then go away and let it all percolate. For an infant whose mother was an editor, I came up with a word theme," she recalls, "spelling out a nursery rhyme in calligraphy and punctuating it with a couple of images." Another design she did for a little girl has been requested by many of the parents who saw it. Vines of ivy flow around the room, up and down the walls. To keep it lively, Bereczki makes the ivy "disappear" into a closet, then come out the other side. This effect can also be created with bouquets of flowers connected by ribbons, she says. "There is so much competition from wallcovering companies that I have to come up with something unique and interesting."

creative inspiration

Find a mural painter through word-of-mouth or references from paint stores or baby-furnishings shops. Or talk to art students at a local college about doing the work.

OPPOSITE Classic nursery rhymes and fairy tales provide good subject matter for murals.

ABOVE RIGHT Toddlers and older children are intrigued by murals that tell a story.

BELOW LEFT AND RIGHT Stimulate your baby's mind with bright colors and simple but bold patterns.

the story on storage

Storage for a baby? It may sound incongruous, but newborns accumulate a great many possessions in a very short time. Without sufficient storage, the nursery would soon become cluttered and chaotic. In addition to providing a landing spot for clothing, bedding, and diapers, a well-designed nursery must hold a wide range of other baby accessories. Many storage options exist, from stand-alone pieces, such as chests, armoires, and toy boxes, to built-in drawers, cubbies, and shelving—with or without doors.

Furniture for babies comes in all styles, from traditional, to vintage, to modern. You can choose, as many people do, a sweet, old-fashioned look, but this is far from a hard-and-fast rule. In fact, a recent survey of adults who plan to have children revealed that more than half are tired of the overdecorated "baby theme-park" nursery, preferring instead that baby's room be more of a stylish extension of the decor in the rest of their home.

The centerpiece of the nursery will be the crib, cradle, or bassinet. (See Chapter 5, page 112.) Storage furniture—otherwise known as case goods—is available as built-in, modular, or freestanding units. The furniture industry uses a variety of labels regulated by the Federal Trade Commission to inform consumers about the materials used in a piece of case-goods furniture.

- **Solid wood** means that the exposed surfaces are made of the wood specified, without any veneer or plywood. You may see a label saying "solid oak" or "solid pine." Other woods may be used on unexposed surfaces, such as the backs and sides of drawers.
- **Genuine wood** means that all exposed parts of the furniture are made of a veneer (a thin layer) of wood applied over hardwood or plywood.
- **Wood** means that no part of the furniture is made of plastic, metal, or other material.
- **Man-made materials** refers to plastic laminate panels that are printed to look like wood. This furniture may also include plastic molded to resemble wood carving or trim.

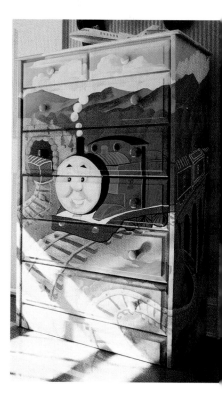

LEFT This creative storage scheme makes good use of a dollhouse-inspired shelving unit. With the door removed, a closet offers easy access to necessities.

RIGHT A bureau decorated with a favorite cartoon character will delight a toddler.

you don't need to be a professional designer to furnish your baby's new space. To guarantee the best results, however, it wouldn't hurt to follow a few simple guidelines. Keeping these basics in mind will enhance your expertise and confidence.

Start by measuring. Using a steel measuring tape, measure and record the dimensions of the room and the size of any openings—the door into the room, closet doors, windows, and so forth. Record, too, the measurements of permanent features, such as built-in dressers or shelves. Note the positions of electrical switches and outlets, light fixtures, phone jacks, radiators, heat registers, air ducts, or vents. If you have already planned to use certain pieces of furniture, measure those, too.

Draw a freehand sketch of the baby's room, using the measurements you've made and incorporating all of the room's elements noted above.

Next, **create a floor plan.** There are a number of free programs on the Web that allow you to arrange furniture right on your computer screen. You can also transfer the sketch to graph paper. You'll need a ruler or straightedge, a sharp pencil, and an eraser for drawing your floor plan. A plan drawn to scale will be an invaluable reference when it's time for you to lay out the room or shop for furniture. To keep your sketch neat and accurate, use quad-ruled graph paper with four squares to the inch. The squares are small enough to make the finished sketch manageable but large enough to let you easily place various furniture templates.

develop
a plan

Using your initial rough sketch as a guide, copy your measurements onto the graph paper, letting each square equal one foot. Then, figure out what pieces of furniture you will need for the baby's room and draw these on your floor plan. Don't guess about furniture sizes—it can lead to costly mistakes. Salespeople can provide you with exact sizes for the furniture you may be buying.

Spend some time trying out different furniture arrangements on the plan, creating a focal point by positioning the largest piece first. Also remember the design principles discussed on pages 10-17.

you needn't be a pro to create a great look

Because the nursery will probably evolve into a toddler's room, choose storage that baby can use later, such as child-height shelves in the closet and a chest of drawers with easy-pull handles.

Whether it's a nursery, a toddler's room, or a teenager's sanctuary, put safety first and bolt bookcases and other tall pieces of furniture to the wall.

RIGHT Just about any kind of dresser can be put into service now as a changing table and used later as storage for an older child's room.

how much will you need?

How do you know whether a room will be too crowded? Will there be enough space to open the drawers under a changing table if you place it near the door? Can you fit the crib against one wall and still have room for a chest? Here are some rules of thumb on clearances of items typically found in a baby's room.

- Maintain 40 inches of space into the room to open drawers without blocking a traffic aisle.
- Reserve 3 feet of space in front of a closet to allow the door to open easily.
- Keep 22 inches of clear space around the crib.
- Leave 6 inches between furniture pieces and baseboard heating and air-conditioning units.
- Finally, don't forget to allow room for access to wall outlets and light switches.

good investment

Plan now for the future by installing a sturdy, adjustable bookshelf that will hold stuffed animals for a baby, puzzles and toys for a child, books and media equipment for a teenager.

what's in wood furniture?

Furniture can be constructed of several different wood materials:

- **Hardwoods** are from deciduous trees, such as cherry, maple, oak, ash, pecan, teak, walnut, mahogany, and poplar. These woods are often used in high-quality furniture because of their strength and durability.
- **Softwoods** are from conifer trees, including fir, pine, redwood, cedar, and cypress. These woods must be well seasoned and kiln dried before lumber is used, or it will split and splinter easily.
- **Veneers** are thin sheets of hardwood that are glued to a core of less-expensive material, such as plywood or particleboard. Veneers were once associated with poor-quality furniture, but veneer furniture made today is more acceptable and may be stronger than solid wood. Wide boards of solid wood can warp and crack, but veneer over plywood won't.

Inspect joining methods to evaluate how the furniture is made. Look for strong construction at the joints. Most furniture is glued together, fastened with screws, or a combination of the two. Staples are often used on poor-quality pieces. Avoid these, especially if the furniture will bear weight.

choose high-quality wood pieces

ABOVE LEFT A flea-market find or a treasure from your own attic might be just what's needed for your child's room.

LEFT This contemporary changing table-dresser combination was designed especially for the nursery.

OPPOSITE This built-in unit, with desk, drawers, and shelves, can accommodate a child's growing needs.

built-in furniture

If the nursery is oddly shaped, built-in furniture is a particularly good choice because it can be custom made for the space. The downside is that custom-made furniture can be expensive. Before you decide whether this is a worthwhile option for you, get several estimates from reputable carpenters in your area. If you decide to go ahead with built-ins, check the carpenter's references carefully—preferably by talking to people you know and trust who have worked with this professional before. Also, be sure to look at examples of the carpenter's work, examining it closely, and ask for an estimate in writing. Make sure the estimate includes items such as knobs, hinges, and other hardware, which can create an expensive surprise if not addressed up front.

freestanding pieces

As the name implies, freestanding furniture stands alone and is not attached to or supported by other pieces. Individual furniture pieces may be part of a matched set with a common finish, detailing, and hardware, but they usually can be purchased separately. Several freestanding pieces that do not match can create a more lively, interesting look than a suite of furniture.

Dressers and chests are classified by how much they can hold. They include, from the smallest to largest, the lingerie chest, drawer chest, door chest, and armoire. The first two types feature only drawers while the door chest has both drawers and doors. The armoire may have a hanging rod or shelves inside.

At first you'll be able to get by with only a small chest; but as your child grows so will her clothing-storage needs. If space and budget permit, invest in a large dresser or armoire now.

Go Green

An old but charming garage-sale dresser can serve as both a storage piece and a focal point in the nursery. Just give it a fresh coat of paint—nontoxic, of course.

ABOVE LEFT In this contemporary bedroom, low shelves with easy-to-open storage doors place a toddler's toys within easy reach.

OPPOSITE BELOW To make a flea market find—such as this lingerie chest—perfect for baby's room, give it a quick decorating makeover with a new coat of paint and decals or stencils.

RIGHT This modern bookcase features deep shelves for tucking in a toddler's favorite stuffed animals for the night. Clean, contemporary styling makes this piece especially versatile.

modular furniture

Modular systems consist of separate, coordinated units that can be purchased individually or as an entire suite. Modular systems look very much like built-ins but, unless custom made, are more affordable. The price is determined by the number of pieces you buy and the finish you choose. If assembly is required, you'll have to factor in that cost, too, unless you do it yourself. To determine whether a do-it-yourself approach works for you, ask the salesperson what level of skill you should have and what tools you will need.

should you buy a vintage crib?

Vintage cribs are available at many antique stores, flea markets, and even garage sales. Depending upon their quality and condition, they can be less expensive than a new one, and can have a charming, nostalgic appeal. Nice idea, but those simpler times were also more dangerous for babies. Although a vintage crib may be sturdier than a new budget model—and possibly more stylish—it probably does not meet today's standards for safety. Unless you're prepared to modify an older piece so that its construction and finish are compliant with CPSC safety guidelines, opt instead for buying something new and safe that is sleek and contemporary or a reproduction patterned after a vintage design.

check it out

Before you buy baby furniture— new or old—check it for sturdiness and look for strong hinges and supports. Run your hands across all visible parts, making sure the finish is smooth. Check, too, for rough edges or sharp corners. If possible, choose pieces with rounded corners so that sharp edges are never a problem.

Make sure shelving is strong and adjustable. Avoid any piece with glass doors. Glass that can shatter is a safety hazard, of course, but even if the glass is shatterproof you'll have to wipe it clean frequently as it becomes finger-smudged.

OPPOSITE BOTTOM Repainted with wide, neutral stripes and a charming mural, this antique chest of drawers will be useful and appealing for years to come.

ABOVE If you've got a yen for nostalgia, a vintage crib may be a good choice for you. They're readily available in antique shops and flea markets, and sometimes turn up at garage sales, too. Before you buy, make sure the crib meets safety criteria.

how to find more room

no matter how much storage the individual pieces of furniture in baby's room provide, it doesn't hurt to have just a little bit more. Even in a small nursery, you can create additional storage by using your imagination.

First, think outside the box—a closet or bureau isn't the only place to store clothes. Consider installing one or more racks with pegs for hanging frequently used items, or add an old coat tree that you have painted to match the room. Baby clothes are too cute to stow away—keep them on display.

Study the room for other clever storage possibilities in corners, under eaves, and on walls. These are perfect areas for built-ins, which increase storage capacity without using up precious floor space. Take a look at the closet, too. If it's a standard design it's probably a big space-waster, with an empty area under those little outfits hanging on the one-and-only rod. Utilize the wasted space by stacking plastic containers on the floor and filling them with extra clothes, bed linens, or diapers. Another idea—put up a second rod, lower than the first, and hang more clothes on that. It will soon be reachable for your child as he grows and is able to hang up his own clothes.

Wicker baskets provide enormous decorative and practical versatility. Other pieces specifically designed for a variety of storage needs include rolling carts and shelving units, either wall-mounted or freestanding. Such items are manufactured in a wide array of sizes, colors, and materials. Some may work well as is, while others may need some decorative modifications such as painting or re-covering.

Finally, don't limit your thinking to items sold specifically for storage. Browse through crafts stores, antique shops, and garage sales for hat boxes, toy chests, and trunks, which you can spruce up with paint or re-cover with fabric or leftover wallpaper. Vintage suitcases, which can be filled with extra items and stacked, are also widely available.

ABOVE Small toys create clutter and pose safety hazards in the nursery. Tuck them away on the inside or outside of a closet door in an over-the-door shoe rack.

RIGHT Quick storage—fill a basket with toys, and slide it under the crib.

buyer beware

A high price does
not always mean
high quality. Carefully
check each piece of
furniture, no matter
how expensive,
before buying.

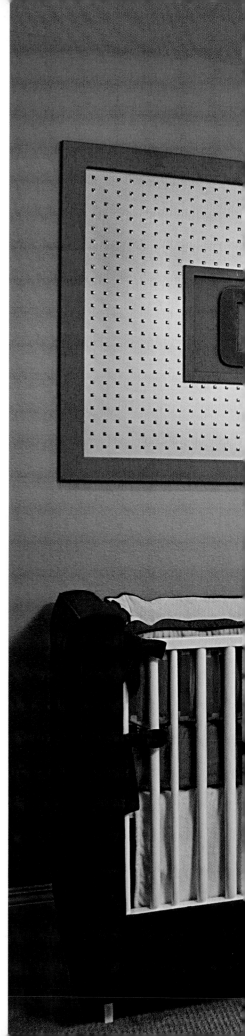

Walls, Windows, and Floors

Chances are that the walls, floors, and windows of the nursery may need a little attention before baby arrives. Don't worry. It doesn't cost much for some paint or a few rolls of wallcovering—and a couple of hours' work can transform a once-drab room into a cozy, colorful space. Do you need to replace the floor? That can be an easy and economical project, too. There are many options for nursery floors, including some that you can quickly and easily install yourself.

- **creative ways with walls**
- **window treatments**
- **planning the view**
- **flooring options**

Create design appeal by highlighting one wall with bold color and dramatic art.

your choices for walls, windows, and floors can work together to create the look and ambiance you want for baby's first room. Even if your funds are limited, you can find a wide selection of affordable options that come in standard sizes and are ready for on-the-spot installation. Walls in particular can provide a neutral background against which to view the nursery's other highlights. You can also let the walls dominate the room's design by choosing bold wallcovering or a hand-painted mural that tells a story.

Before deciding on a specific wallpaper pattern or paint color, think about the style of furniture you're planning to use in the room. Is it strictly functional, a bit whimsical, or a mixed bag? If the furniture is highly decorative on its own, choose subtle patterns and colors so that the walls won't compete for attention. Conversely, you may want to use a striking design to create the visual interest

creative ways with walls

that plain, understated furniture cannot offer. An effective wall treatment may also help visually pull disparate elements of the room together by providing a cohesive backdrop for them all.

Paint can transform an ordinary room into a luscious-looking nursery in a few hours—and it's the least expensive way to do so. You don't have to restrict paint to the walls, either—a coat or two can effectively create a complementary look for mismatched, hand-me-down pieces that you may have inherited. Once you've chosen a color you can introduce harmonious shades for accessories such as curtains, bedding, carpets, or rugs.

Some designers advise that you paint the room to please yourself because the baby won't really notice. Other experts cite the ill effects of certain vivid colors and bold patterns on babies and suggest that you choose soothing shades or tiny restful prints. Review the information about color and pattern in Chapter 2; then make the decision that seems most sensible to you. Whatever color you choose, make certain paints and wallcoverings are nontoxic and easy to clean.

OPPOSITE TOP
A collection of vintage shovels in bright colors contrasts with the robin's egg blue of the nursery walls.

RIGHT Bold, simple wall art—in this case, a sign with baby's name—provides visual stimulation for a newborn.

BELOW In most of its hues, green is a restful color for a baby's room.

nighty night

This nursery incorporates a lively wall design on a calm background color that encourages sleep.

how much paint will you need?

Don't get caught short. To estimate the amount of paint you'll need, **1. Multiply the length** of each wall by its height. **2. Add the walls** together. **3. Multiply the height** of each door and window by its width. **4. Subtract the door and window** area from the wall area. **5. If there are built-in features,** such as bookcases, measure them in the same way and subtract them as well. **6. To estimate the quantity** of paint you'll need, divide the adjusted total by 300 square feet. (Most paint companies say that a gallon of paint will cover 350 to 400 square feet.) **7. Multiply this figure by 2** if you plan to apply two coats. There should be enough leftover paint for touching up later, if necessary.

paint ideas

Applying a wonderful color that pleases you and your family will go a long way toward making the nursery special. If you're unsure about choosing a color, refer to the suggestions and ideas in Chapter 2. Color is a very personal choice, but a little bit of knowledge about how various colors "feel," what they suggest, how they might affect the baby, and how they work alone or in combination with each other will give you confidence and help you create a pleasing design scheme.

OPPOSITE Rather than using traditional colors, such as pink or blue, many parents choose pale yellow for the nursery. The shade here is light enough to qualify as a neutral but offers more punch.

RIGHT An old dresser updated with a coat of paint in a rich buttercream color adds cheer to the nursery.

the economics of paint

Painting is the least-expensive way to add color and personality to the walls, but only if you shop wisely and remember some basic points.

● **Paint grades.** Don't skimp. Better-quality paints tend to cost more, but don't count out the high-grade products. Low-cost and—usually—lower-quality paints are not always a bargain. They often don't provide the coverage that a higher-quality paint does, so you may need to use additional coats. The extra gallons you'll buy will eat up those savings quickly.

● **Nontoxic formula.** According to the Environmental Protection Agency (EPA), standard interior wallpaint is a prime source of indoor pollution because it emits toxic VOCs (Volatile Organic Compounds) long after its initial application. Look for low-VOC paint made from natural ingredients, such as water, milk, and plants, for baby's room.

● **Paint finish.** Paint with a flat (nonreflective) finish is usually fine, but it won't hold up in a child's room. Unless you plan to repaint the room often, consider investing in paint with one of these finishes: eggshell (slight sheen); satin (a bit more luster); semigloss (slightly glossy and light reflective); or gloss (produces a hard, shiny finish). These finishes are more expensive than flat paints, but they are easier to clean with a damp cloth and mild detergent.

dual decision

Can't decide between paint and wallcovering? Use both. Apply a stylish paint shade to nursery walls; then top them with a removable wall appliqué.

BELOW Brown in the nursery? Why not? It's warm and sophisticated without being too stimulating for an infant.

OPPOSITE An eye-catching mural that tells a simple story aids baby's mental and visual development.

avoid confusion

In case you've wondered, the term "wallpaper" is often used interchangeably with "wallcovering," even when the material has no (or very little) actual paper in it.

wallcovering

Wallcoverings come in several forms and an array of patterns and colors.

- **Paper-backed vinyl** wallcoverings are washable and peelable; the latter feature is particularly desirable because it allows quick removal when it's time to update the room. Paper-backed vinyl is frequently sold prepasted, which makes it quicker to install. Most wallcoverings for nurseries and kids' rooms are of this type for practical reasons.
- **Fabric-backed vinyl** features a vinyl top layer over fiberglass or cloth. It's heavier than paper-backed products and stands up well to the scrubbing needed to remove tough marks and stains. The downside? Fabric-backed vinyl is not available prepasted.
- **Vinyl-coated papers** are less expensive and less resistant to stains than the other two types.

how much will you need?

To estimate your wallcovering needs, you will need to take some measurements using a steel measuring tape. First, measure wall height from floor to ceiling, excluding baseboards and moldings. Measure the length of each wall, including doors and windows. Take measurements in feet, rounding off to the next highest half foot or foot. If hanging the entire room, add all wall length measurements to get the perimeter. Find the total square feet of the wall(s) by multiplying wall height by room perimeter. Subtract areas such as doors and windows that will not be covered. This will give you the total number of square feet to be covered. You can then determine how many rolls to order.

OPPOSITE Oversize pink flowers charmingly bedeck a little girl's bathroom. The vinyl-coated wallcovering easily stands up to the moisture and humidity of the room.

OPPOSITE BOTTOM AND BELOW, LEFT AND RIGHT Wallcovering can be a more expensive choice than paint—and not quite as easy to change. So a practical choice for a nursery might be a background that isn't too juvenile. You can always add or change a border to make it more age appropriate.

borders

Wallpaper borders come in a huge array of designs. You can make use of them in a nursery or toddler's room either by matching—or contrasting—with the overall pattern you have chosen or as a stand-alone design element. The latter is a good choice if you've decided to go with a more subdued nursery decor.

A cheerful border paired with a paint color that pleases you may be all you need to create a pretty room for baby. Borders are typically applied high, where the wall and ceiling intersect, but some designers suggest applying them 30 inches above the floor—about chair-rail height—to provide an interesting visual for baby to gaze at from his crib.

picking a pattern

There are a dizzying number of wallpaper patterns available these days, many of them designed expressly for babies' rooms. Popular themes include nursery-rhyme and cartoon characters, animals, alphabets, numbers—and of course—hearts, flowers, bunnies, kittens, and other cute animals. Because the general rule is to refrain from overstimulating an infant, it is probably best to choose a small-scale nursery pattern with a background in a soothing color. To add interest without overwhelming the room, get creative with wallpaper borders. You can be a bit more adventurous for a toddler, making use of the bolder prints, patterns, and murals offered by some wallpaper companies.

OPPOSITE TOP Any wallpaper border that baby enjoys looking at is a good choice.

RIGHT Borders designed to coordinate with wallcoverings make decorating a breeze.

BELOW This wallpaper design is just the thing for a little boy's room—a lively border of cars, buses, and best of all, trucks.

window treatments

indow treatments—an interior designer's phrase for anything that covers and dresses up a window, such as a curtain, drapery, blind, shade, or shutter—serve several important functions. They modulate the light so that baby can nap any time of day; they draw attention to attractive windows and highlight lovely outdoor vistas; and conversely, they camouflage awkwardly shaped windows and disguise unsightly views. Window treatments are also a decorative tool. They serve as a vehicle for bringing color and pattern into the room, often helping to pull together all the other decorative elements such as wallpaper, upholstery, rugs, and flooring. In addition, some types of window treatments also allow you to effectively control the amount of natural light and air that enter the room, which is especially important in a nursery.

Depending on how they are constructed, some window treatments provide insulation as well. In areas of the country where summers are very hot and winters very cold, this feature is important for baby's comfort. For maximum flexibility, you might consider combining or layering two or more types of treatments. For example, hang filmy, sheer curtains, which diffuse and soften light, with lined draperies or over room-darkening shades. With a combination such as this, you can make the nursery cheerful, light, and airy when baby wants to play, or dim and cozy when it's nap time. Another window design might combine a soft treatment, such as a valance or swag, hung over hard-edged blinds or shutters.

Before you make a decision about this important decorative element, take into account your overall color scheme, wall and ceiling finishes, floor covering, and the look and style of the furniture. Window treatments look best when they coordinate with all of these elements.

If your nursery windows are not a standard size, you may need a custom-designed treatment, which could be pricey. But for standard windows, almost any type of window treatment is available and ready for quick installation, and some can be quite economical.

get creative

Dress up plain-Jane window shades with wallpaper, iron-on fabric, decals, or even designs you create yourself with fabric paint.

OPPOSITE Whether you choose curtains, shades, or blinds for the nursery's windows, make sure you are able to block bright sunlight when it's time for the baby to nap.

RIGHT When closed, these blinds effectively keep out the light. They also provide a playful panorama of tropical birds to delight baby.

planning the view

t o make your window treatments all you want them to be, take some tips from design experts.

- **Look outside.** Is the view framed by the nursery windows worth highlighting, or should it be downplayed? What about the window itself? Fussy treatments tend to draw attention to windows, but simpler styles allow you to focus attention on other elements in the room.
- **Follow the sun.** Exposure to the sun at various times during the day will affect the color palette of the room. This is because the way colors are perceived changes according to the light and determines the amount of room darkening and insulation you will need. If one or more windows face east, you may want to block morning sun. West-facing windows will get afternoon sun, which in summer will be hot and bright. Windows with a northern exposure won't receive direct sunlight, which means in winter there will be no warming rays. A south-facing room receives sunlight most of the day.
- **Select the right hardware.** Mounting a window treatment inside the frame requires careful measuring—you want a secure fit for your rod or pole. An outside mount allows more flexibility—you can use any type of hardware, and you can mount the rod on the window frame or the wall. If the hardware will be visible, make sure its style suits the decor of the nursery. Use a sufficiently sturdy rod to insure that the curtain drapes properly.
- **Measure everything.** Even if they look the same, don't assume that all of the nursery windows have the same measurements. Use a steel measuring tape, and record the exact dimensions for every window in the room.
- **What price maintenance?** Consider your long-term budget before deciding to go with custom-made treatments or delicate or special-care fabrics and trim because they require expensive professional cleaning.

In this south-facing nursery, heavy, lined draperies were necessary to control heat and light from the sun.

window treatments play

both a decorative and functional role in the nursery

curtains and valances

Curtains and valances are so widely available that you will have no trouble finding what you want. Curtains come long, short, plain, ruffled, and in every color and pattern imaginable. Valances are equally varied—swags, poufs, balloons, festoons, and more. Ruffles and other fancy features generally look best in traditional and country interiors; tailored or simple treatments look good anywhere, including contemporary-style rooms.

With a baby in the house, time and energy will be limited, so choose easy-care materials. Because curtains collect dust, it's essential that you keep them clean and fresh. The easiest fabrics to maintain are cotton-synthetic blends. They're washable, require little or no ironing, and won't fade in the sun. If the curtains you choose are not washable, you'll have to factor professional cleaning bills into your budget. If your baby has allergies, all-natural cotton is a better choice.

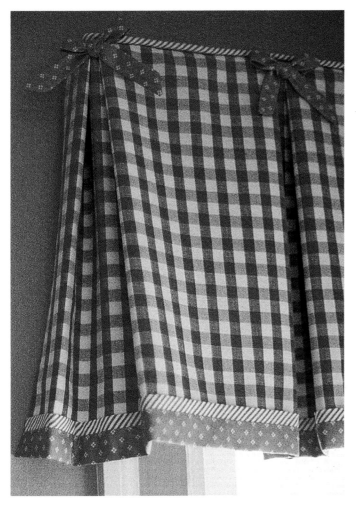

OPPOSITE A valance is typically used with a pair of curtains, but this fresh green gingham design is distinctive enough to stand alone.

LEFT Crib draperies that match the window treatments provide extra protection from drafts and elegantly highlight the crib and its precious contents.

BELOW These white shutters lend a crisp yet traditional aura to the nursery. An accompanying valance softens the clean lines.

shutters

Louvered shutters are a versatile way to provide privacy and control light and air in the nursery. The shutter itself can be opened or closed; the louvers can be adjusted to direct a breeze up or down or admit more, or less, light. Shutters can be painted or stained and some come with a panel that allows you to install fabric to match colors and patterns used elsewhere in the room. Like blinds and shades, shutters come in a variety of standard sizes, or they can be custom made for any size windows.

shades

Although economical and widely available, traditional window shades—a single piece of fabric or vinyl attached to a roller—are less attractive and interesting than fabric shades, which come in flat, gathered, or pleated styles. Fabric shades include Roman, balloon, and cellular types, and all of them pack considerably more design punch than the unembellished kind.

Depending on the material from which they are made, some shades filter the sun; others block it completely when tightly drawn. To ensure that the shades will fit tightly enough to block light that might disturb baby's sleep, measure your windows carefully before you go shade shopping.

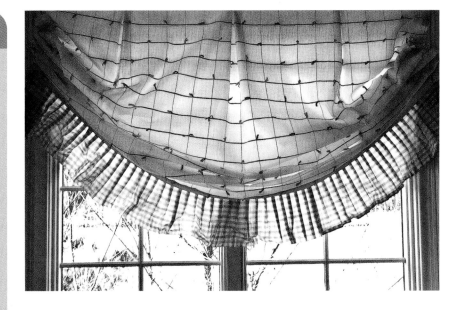

ABOVE In a shady room there may be no need for blinds or curtains, but a pretty valance is always a welcome touch.

BELOW Room-darkening shades prevent glare from disturbing nap time and help keep the room cool on summer days.

OPPOSITE In a little girl's room, horizontal white blinds contrast smartly with fanciful pink wallcovering and pretty bed linens.

Go Green

Is climate control an issue in your part of the country? If so, ask about the insulation level, or R-value, of window treatments before you buy.

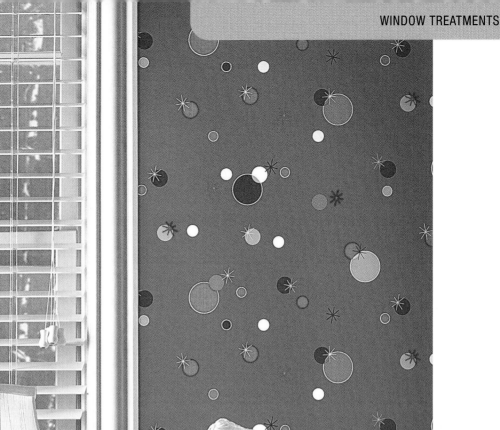

the clean-lined versatility of blinds

The best thing about blinds is their versatility—some types can block sun almost completely; others filter light while allowing ventilation. These handy items come in metal, wood, vinyl, or textured fabric; in vertical or horizontal configurations; and with standard-, mini-, or micro-size slat widths. Wood blinds are available in several finishes, and the other materials come in a wide array of colors and textures. Except for the stained-wood variety, which has a handsome English-library sort of appeal, blinds are potentially sterile looking unless you soften them with curtains or valances.

To keep the nursery as dust-free as possible, clean blinds frequently with the upholstery attachment of your vacuum cleaner. It's a tedious procedure, but it's easier than scrubbing blinds in the bathtub.

To guarantee a tight, light-blocking fit for window treatments, take precise measurements of your windows—and photos, if possible—along with you when you go shopping.

ABOVE A plethora of pattern makes this window seat cozy and inviting.

RIGHT This striped valance is color-cued to the paint color on the walls.

OPPOSITE In a creative reversal of the usual order, this toddler's room features wallpaper below a chair rail and a painted wall above it.

windows 1,2,3

If your decorating budget for the nursery is a little bit tight, consider planning your window treatments so that they can be purchased and implemented in three easy stages.

- **Stage One** has a practical goal and addresses the most important concerns: to control light and provide privacy. Blinds, shades, and shutters are the most obvious, effective, and economical options to meet this need.

- **Stage Two** is the time to begin dressing up the windows to complement the overall look of the room. For this, a good-looking curtain rod and curtain panels will do nicely. Just be sure to choose a pattern and color that harmonizes with your other fabrics and accessories.

- **Stage Three** offers you a final opportunity to add a special detail or two, such as a shaped cornice, a coordinated valance, or pretty tiebacks. Be careful, however, that your choices are safe ones for the nursery and don't contain objects that can harm the baby.

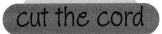

cut the cord

Beware—the cords on certain types of blinds and shades pose a safety hazard for little ones. Never let them dangle where babies or toddlers can grab them.

your flooring options

the room you have designated as the nursery may already have a perfectly good floor. If not, it's a good idea to do some serious planning now so that you'll have the right flooring in place before the baby arrives.

As you review the options here, keep in mind that some flooring materials can be mixed and matched for design interest, provided the floor does not end up out of harmony with the walls and other elements of the room.

Wood flooring is a traditional favorite. It's available in narrow strips 2 to 3 inches wide, all the way to 10-inch-wide farmhouse-style planks, with many configurations in between. Another possibility is wood parquet, a rich, perennially popular look. And thanks to advanced manufacturing techniques, laminate flooring provides the look of wood for a fraction of the cost.

What's best—hardwood or softwood? Hardwoods, such as maple, oak, birch, or ash, can stand up to normal wear-and-tear, but they are costly and won't tolerate abuse. Softwoods, such as pine and fir, while not recommended for high-traffic areas such as a kitchen, may be suitable for a nursery or toddler's room.

Both hardwoods and softwoods are graded according to their grain, color, and imperfections. The top grade is clear, followed by select, number-1 common, and number-2 common. You'll want to consider cost when deciding which grade of wood to use, but do consider other factors. For instance, if you plan to sand the floor, treat it with polyurethane, and leave much of it exposed, it's important to choose one of the better grades. Are you going to stain your wood floor? Imperfections are less noticeable with darker stains. Natural wood stains range from very light ash to deep coffee tones. The darker shades create a formal, traditional aura, while lighter stains tend to make a room feel casual and modern. Colored stains, such as reds, blues, and greens—also impart a casual, even whimsical feel that may be just right for baby's room.

Maintaining a wood floor is easy if it has been properly sealed. Polyurethane creates a durable finish and is easy to apply. Usually all that is required after sealing is regular vacuuming or dust mopping.

LEFT Baby will spend a lot of time playing on the floor, so make sure your choice is attractive but easy to clean.

RIGHT If you want to avoid carpeting the entire nursery, think about using a large area rug, such as this one. Its soft texture and playful design will delight both babies and toddlers.

resilient vinyl flooring

An easy-on-the-budget option for the nursery is resilient-vinyl flooring. It's reasonably priced and easy to keep clean—an attractive feature for a baby's room. Some types can be installed by a relatively inexperienced do-it-yourselfer, which also helps keep costs down. Cushioned sheet vinyl—comfortable and quiet underfoot—is the most comfortable choice. Other types come in both sheets and tiles, and all are available in a huge range of colors and patterns. You'll have no trouble finding a floor to suit your nursery decor.

To keep vinyl flooring looking good, just sweep and damp mop it regularly. Stain-resistant and no-wax finishes make some types even easier to maintain.

frugal flooring

You'll be amazed at the deep discount you can get for a carpet remnant. For a small charge, many stores will even bind the remnant to give it a finished look.

Go Green

Cork and linoleum are natural, eco-friendly flooring materials that are also sturdy, comfortable, and easy to maintain.

laminate flooring

OPPOSITE An "area rug" made from linoleum tiles covers cork flooring in this child's room.

ABOVE Whatever material you choose for your child's floor—wood, vinyl, carpet, or this wood-patterned laminate—make sure it's durable and easy care. A clean floor is essential for baby's health.

If the expense of a real wood floor threatens to break the budget, consider laminate, a wood lookalike that resists stains and scratches and is often given a warranty for up to 15 years against cracking, peeling, and scarring. However, laminate products vary in both price and quality. Less-expensive versions may not hold up well to excessive wear.

Laminate flooring comes in a variety of wood tones and other designs, is easy to keep clean, and can be applied over virtually any surface—wood, concrete, sheet vinyl, vinyl tile, or ceramic tile. Looking for a do-it-yourself project? Laying a laminate floor can be a quick, economical choice for a reasonably handy person.

hide the dirt

Shopping for carpets or area rugs for the nursery? Consider multicolored patterns—they're excellent for camouflaging soil and stains.

carpet and rugs

Available in perhaps even more colors, patterns, and styles than resilient flooring—and definitely in more sizes—carpeting and rugs can easily meet any budget and design need. For example, wall-to-wall carpeting provides a soft, warm surface on which baby can crawl, and it offers a rich, textured look that can beautifully complement the decor of any room. Scatter rugs with nonslip adhesive backings are both useful and versatile. Whatever type of rug you choose, make certain that the surface is suitable for baby's room.

Carpeting is also available in a variety of materials and textures. Wool is the most durable—and expensive—and also has the advantage of being naturally fire resistant. Carpeting made from synthetic fibers offers the greatest variety in color, pattern, and texture and is more affordable in the short term, although not as durable as wool over time. A wool-synthetic blend, which combines many of the best features of both these types of fibers, is a good compromise, offering a reasonably wide variety of design options, enhanced durability, and some savings over the price of pure wool.

To keep most carpets fresh and in good condition, vacuum them regularly, wipe up spills immediately, and clean them periodically with a steam or shampoo machine.

Make use of area rugs to create separate play and sleep areas within the baby's room or to divide the space into feeding and dressing zones. Area rugs can be an inexpensive way to add accent colors that help tie the overall decorating scheme together. For safety, make sure all of the area rugs you buy for your child's room are backed with a nonskid material.

OPPOSITE Rugs and carpets offer a forgiving surface for baby's early adventures. Low-to-the ground furniture, soft toys, and plenty of pillows also prevent injuries.

LEFT To make maintenance easier, place a small, washable area rug on top of wall-to-wall carpeting.

BELOW This plush area rug features whimsical raised "dots" in cheerful colors.

Go Green

Choose carpeting, window treatments, and bedding made from natural fibers, such as cotton or wool, which are free of toxins and pesticides.

many nurseries now boast a contemporary

removing carpet stains

Even before the baby starts to crawl, the carpet in her room can become soiled and stained by debris tracked in on shoes, spots from the baby oil container that was accidentally kicked onto the floor, or spills from the baby bottle that the sitter dropped. Here are some rules for removing spots and stains successfully.

1. Clean up a spot or spill immediately.
2. Use white cloths or paper towels.
3. Blot a stain—never rub or scrub.
4. Work from the outer edge in toward the center of the spot.
5. Follow up with clean water to remove any residue of the stain.
6. Blot any remaining moisture by layering white paper towels over the spot and weighing them down with a heavy object.

- **Water-soluble stains.** Blot as much as possible with paper towels that have been dampened in cold water. If necessary, mix a solution of ¼ teaspoon of clear, mild, nonbleach laundry detergent with one quart of water, and spray it lightly onto the spot. Blot repeatedly with white paper towels. Rinse with a spray of clean water; then blot dry.

- **Urine or vomit.** Mix equal parts of white vinegar and water, and blot onto the spot with white paper towels. Then clean with detergent solution.

- **Oil-based stains** (cosmetics, ink, paint, shoe polish). Blot as much as possible. Then, wearing rubber gloves to protect your hands, apply a nonflammable spot remover made specifically for grease, oil, or tar to a clean, white paper towel. Blot the stain with the treated towel.

- **Blood, cola, or chocolate.** Apply a solution of 1 tablespoon of ammonia and 1 cup of water to the stain; then go over it with a detergent solution. Don't use ammonia on a wool carpet; instead, try an acid stain remover, such as lemon juice or white vinegar diluted with water.

color palette

OPPOSITE The area rug's orange-color band is picked up in other nursery accents.

ABOVE Small area rugs can be tossed in the washing machine; other types are treated to resist stains.

5

Keeping Baby Cozy

The nursery is a special place, unlike any other room in the house. For the first few months of your new baby's life, this room will be used for little more than sleeping, nursing, and diaper changing. Despite what some stores and interior designers might lead you to believe, baby's needs are few—at first. If you have the budget and the inclination to fill the room with luxuries, that's fine—and you'll probably have fun doing it. But it is not really necessary. As long as you have the basics, baby is on the way to being happy and contented.

- sweet dreams
- mattress and bedding
- changing table options
- chairs and mobiles

The number-one priority in the nursery is a safe and comfortable place for baby to sleep.

sweet dreams

f or the first few months, your baby will spend most of every day sleeping. The typical newborn sleeps about 16 to 18 hours out of every 24, waking every two to four hours to be fed. Between 1 month and 2 years of age a baby's total sleep time gradually decreases, down to about 13 hours.

Basically, babies sleep when they want, and there is not much you can do to make them fall asleep—or to wake them. However, it is true that most babies will sleep best in a quiet, darkened room. Although you might find it convenient to install a night-light for wee-hour feedings and changings, the baby is fine sleeping in the dark, and in fact may sleep better without a light. Little ones don't usually become afraid of the dark until 2 or 3 years of age, when they are able to imagine "scary things" under the bed.

Sleeping options for your newborn include a cradle, a crib, a bassinet, and of course, your own bed. Some new parents choose "co-sleeping," keeping the baby in bed with them for the first few weeks. This is a controversial practice—some pediatricians and child-safety experts believe that co-sleeping increases the risk of Sudden Infant Death Syndrome (SIDS); others say the evidence for this danger is weak; still others argue that co-sleeping actually reduces the risk of SIDS. A potentially safer way to keep baby close is a co-sleeper-style crib that opens to your bed on one side, keeping the baby close but not in danger of being squashed if either parent should toss or turn over in sleep. If you decide to share the family bed with your baby—on a conventional mattress; never on a waterbed—check with your pediatrician regarding safety precautions.

To be sure the essentials are in place in plenty of time, you should be thinking about your baby's sleeping arrangements well before your due date. You'll find plenty of information here to help you make your decisions.

This elegant nursery is spacious enough for lucky twin babies. At the end of each crib is a bench with a padded seat cushion; each bench top lifts up to reveal a toy chest, which will be a handy amenity later. The elaborate chest of drawers and gilt-framed mirror are unusual but handsome touches.

nursery essentials

There are many expenses associated with putting together a nursery, and furniture and accessories account for only a portion of the budget. Fortunately, the absolute necessities are few. Start with these basics, and fill in with items you discover later that will make caring for baby easier and more comfortable.

- Crib
- Changing table
- Comfortable chair, rocker, or glider
- Chest of drawers
- Side table
- General lighting
- Flooring
- Table lamp
- Mobile
- Baby monitor

ABOVE Created to look like an antique, this new cradle features a rocking mechanism with a kickstand-style brake.

ABOVE RIGHT Whether you choose a crib or a cradle for baby's first months, make sure construction is sturdy and the spacing between slats meets safety standards.

RIGHT In this fanciful nursery, the crib is shaped like a swan, complete with wings and a long graceful neck.

cradles to gently rock baby to sleep

A cross between a small crib and a rocking chair, a cradle can safely be used for the first four months of baby's life. Usually made of wood, cradles measure roughly 18 x 36 inches. Their side-to-side rocking motion is soothing for babies, which may account for the fact that so many families welcome heirloom cradles that are often passed down from generation to generation. Meaningful as that may be, check a vintage cradle for safety features before using it, and outfit it with a firm new mattress that is at least 2 inches thick.

bassinets

For their first few months, many babies sleep in a bassinet—a light, woven basket that sits in a stand. Choose one that lifts smoothly out of the stand for easy transportation from room to room. A bassinet can also be kept in the nursery during the day and moved to the master bedroom at night for late feedings. Because a bassinet is used only for the first few months, you might consider borrowing one. Just be sure that the mattress is firm and fits snugly; if not, buy a new one.

RIGHT Crib canopies were used hundreds of years ago to keep babies warm in drafty houses. While not necessary today, they do add panache. This canopy creates the look of a circus tent; the giant giraffe reinforces the theme.

OPPOSITE If fanciful isn't your style, you can easily find a contemporary crib with a clean-line look.

crib facts

Even if you use a bassinet or cradle at first, eventually your baby will need a crib. Cribs come in a large variety of sizes, styles, and finishes, and you'll probably make your choice based at least in part on the decor you've chosen for the nursery. Therefore, it's a good idea to plan the overall look of the room ahead of time. While you're planning, you may also want to consider buying a crib that will later convert to a junior bed.

Check cribs for sturdiness and proper assembly, making sure there are no loose slats or carelessly constructed joints. Do not buy a new crib, no matter how attractive the deal, unless it carries a safety certification seal from the Juvenile Products Manufacturers Association (JPMA). Vintage cribs with decorative cutouts and corner-post finials are not considered safe today; neither are slats spaced more than 2½ inches apart. Have the paint tested. If it contains lead, have the paint removed by a certified contractor.

pair streamlined furnishings with vintage pieces

OPPOSITE Proving that decorating a nursery has become more sophisticated, this room juxtaposes up-to-date furniture, bright colors, and contemporary artwork against a vintage-style chandelier and wall sconce.

ABOVE A chair near the crib is a necessity when baby is very young and needs feeding and cuddling during the night. Many parents choose a rocker, but this compact club chair also fills the bill.

sleep safe

To keep babies warm and safe at night, dress them in snuggly sleepers or "wearable blankets"— sack-like garments made of micro-fleece.

mattress and bedding

Whether you choose a brand-new crib or a quaint vintage model, choose a mattress that's snug and firm. According to the Consumer Product Safety Commission (CPSC), the ideal mattress fits tightly (tight enough that you can't slide two fingers between it and the side of the crib) and is firm enough to support the baby's growing body. The tight fit keeps the baby from becoming trapped between the mattress and the crib frame, a possible smothering risk.

Innerspring mattresses generally maintain their shape over the long term better than foam types. If you're shopping for one, ask about the number of coils—for a crib mattress, there should be 150. Foam mattresses, made of polyester or polyether, are light and relatively inexpensive, and come in a variety of thicknesses and densities. The best for baby is a density of roughly 1.5 pounds per cubic foot.

When you're shopping for a mattress, look also at the ticking and the venting. Double- or triple-laminated ticking with nylon reinforcement will resist moisture and stand up to normal use. To keep the mattress fresh, you'll need effective venting, too, which permits air circulation and allows odors to escape. Be sure the mattress you choose has plenty of vent holes.

To keep babies safe, forget any romantic notions of pretty, billowy bedding for the crib. Soft, fluffy blankets, cute little comforters, frilly sheets, and pillows all pose a risk for smothering, and none of them should be placed in the crib with the baby. Overheating and the re-breathing of exhaled car-

bon dioxide have also been linked with SIDS. Always place baby on her back for sleeping and remove toys, pillows, and anything else that interferes with good air circulation.

The best fabrics for baby bedding are tight-weave cotton or cotton blends. Chenille is a poor choice—its soft tufts can be pulled loose and chewed, which presents a risk for gagging and choking.

Crib bumpers, originally created to keep babies from sticking their heads through crib slats, are no longer necessary—new guidelines regulate crib-slat distances and prevent that particular danger. Bumpers are now considered by some experts to be downright dangerous in themselves; according to safety consultants, babies can smother or re-breathe exhaled carbon dioxide if they get too close to the bumpers. Not all experts agree on this danger, so talk to your pediatrician before outfitting your baby's crib.

OPPOSITE TOP Crib hangings are decorative; but for safety's sake, make sure they hang well out of baby's reach.

OPPOSITE BOTTOM AND ABOVE Baby bedding comes in all kinds of patterns; personal touches are nice, too.

today's baby products

new bumper crop

Some parents are now using an alternative to standard crib bumpers—a nylon net cover that ties tightly around the inside of the crib, cushions the slats, and keeps the baby's arms and legs from sticking through.

best bedding

Blankets for the crib should be thin and flat, and fastened securely to minimize the risk of covering baby's head or face.

emphasize function and safety

OPPOSITE AND THIS PAGE
For many years, parents have believed that cushy bumper pads—available in a wide range of colors and patterns to mix and match with bed linens—protected their babies from injury in the crib. Lately, however, some safety experts have urged that bumpers not be used. Not all experts agree, but do talk to your own pediatrician before you buy.

RIGHT AND BELOW
Organic all-cotton bedding features a modern stylized pattern. Pink remains a popular choice for a baby girl.

OPPOSITE TOP
Nowadays, bright colors are as popular for babies as tried-and-true pink or blue.

the best

wander the web

Look online for ideas on how to prepare the nursery. Some manufacturers of baby furniture will send you free booklets loaded with design tips.

bedding for baby is both beautiful and safe

the lowdown

Think about buying a crib that sits close to the floor. Standard crib height is strictly for parents' convenience and, say some safety experts, provides just another place from which a baby can fall.

a baby's needs are few and simple, but a place to change diapers is definitely one of them. You'll be changing diapers up to a dozen times a day—sometimes more—for a couple of years, so it pays to create a space for this little chore that's convenient for you and comfortable and safe for baby.

There are several ways to create the ideal changing area for your particular situation. Many parents opt to buy a piece of furniture expressly designed for this purpose. These pieces typically feature compartments, drawers, or a shelf under the diapering surface where you can keep essentials such as diapers, lotion, wipes, towels, even clothes. Some baby changers offer a flip-top that becomes a standard dresser top when it's turned over. This piece of furniture can then be used as a dresser for an older child. Other changing tables transform into a bookcase. While your child is still an infant, you can store diapers and other necessities on the open shelves. Later, the piece will be useful for toys and books.

If you're short on space or dealing with a very tight budget, you can use the top of a stan-

changing table options

dard chest of drawers, provided it is low enough for you to work comfortably and deep enough for baby. You could also use the top of a bookcase, but it, too, must be the right height and depth. If you're fond of vintage furniture you may find a nice-looking dresser at a flea market or antique shop. Just be sure that whatever piece you convert to a diapering station has no exposed nails or wobbly parts; if the wood looks splintery, sand it smooth, and give it a fresh coat of nontoxic paint. Then visit a baby-product store and buy a changing-table pad for the top of the vintage dresser. If there's room, store supplies on the dresser top, too; if not, keep them nearby in baskets or bins or in the top drawer of the dresser—make sure they're readily accessible.

Another idea—use a bassinet as your diapering station. This solution is particularly useful in a small apartment or house where space for baby furniture is at a premium. Get a sturdy, comfortable changing pad, stock a basket with supplies, and you'll be able to move the bassinet and supplies around the house as needed.

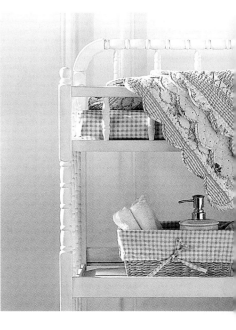

OPPOSITE AND LEFT Top an ordinary bureau with a pad and some supplies, and you've got a changing table for very little money.

BOTTOM LEFT Pretty and practical, an old-fashioned changing table is trimmed with blue-and-white gingham fabric.

BOTTOM RIGHT This changing table can be used later as a bureau for an older child.

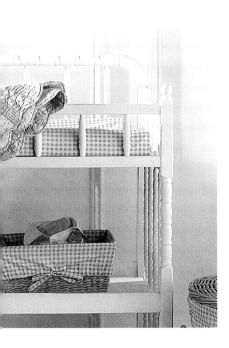

safe diapering

Babies wiggle and squirm when they're being changed— so it's important to keep them safe while you do your work.

- Buy a changing table that stays stable when you shake it. Some experts recommend bolting the table to the wall for extra safety.
- Store everything you need within arm's reach—you'll need to keep one hand on your baby at all times.
- Select a thick, waterproof pad for the table, preferably one with a safety strap. Never leave baby unattended on a changing table.
- Make sure the changing table has a flat, wide surface; high side rails will offer extra protection.

NEAR RIGHT One way to keep the changing table neat and efficient is to stow lotions and other necessities in another spot that's close to hand. Here, charming little galvanized-metal pails do the trick.

FAR RIGHT The ideal diapering station provides storage both closed and open, allowing you to keep some items out of baby's reach and other items easily accessible.

BELOW A portable changing tray goes with you from room to room so that you can diaper baby wherever you are at the moment.

peace and quiet

Before you buy a crib, nursery chair, or other furniture, check each piece for squeaks or grating noises that might disturb baby's sleep. Nursery chairs, for example, should be quiet when you're rocking.

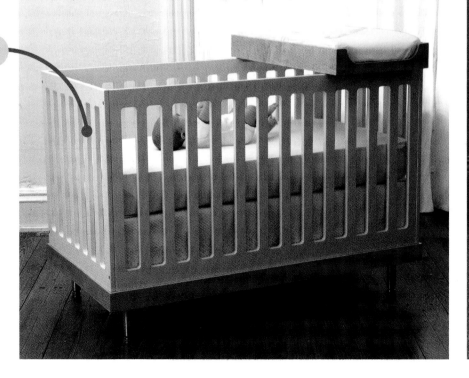

ABOVE In this nursery, an ordinary chest of drawers serves a dual purpose. Drawers store clothes for baby, while the top functions as a diapering station. The contoured pad is shaped to conform to baby's body and is fitted with a removable, washable cover in a plush, comfy material. To keep baby from falling, you should always keep your hand on him while you reach for lotions, powders, and diapers.

OPPOSITE TOP Not a necessity but nice to have, this warming device takes the chill out of baby wipes, an extra comfort for your little one.

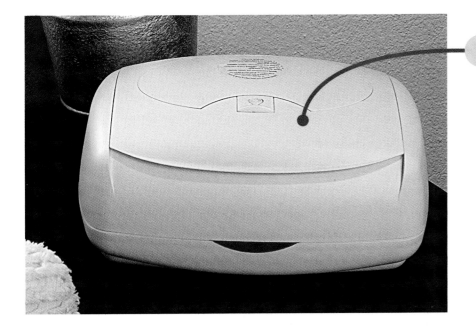

wipes warmer

Some mothers swear by this low-voltage device, set in a plastic housing, that heats from the top down, so that the next baby wipe is always just the right temperature.

dealing with diapers

Diapers are a fact of life for baby's first few years, and it's a good idea to have a workable plan in place well before baby's due date. You'll be dealing with diapers the moment you bring him home. Without a plan, you could easily feel more overwhelmed than you should.

A diaper organizer that holds enough for a day or two and also stores lotions and other sundries will be a big help. You can mount one directly to the changing table so you don't have to take your eyes off baby while you're changing him. Another acceptable method of keeping diapers at hand is to stack them in the compartments that most changing tables offer or to keep them in a basket within easy reach.

You'll also need to deal with soiled diapers, another fact of life. If you're going to subscribe to a diaper service, you'll probably receive a bin for this purpose. For disposable diapers, you'll need your own bin with a sealable, childproof top. A lined deodorized pail, emptied daily, is very serviceable. A more expensive option is a bin that seals each soiled disposable diaper into a plastic bag, which eliminates odors fairly effectively, but it's not very eco-friendly. Another type of container uses a continuous-scented, triple-barrier liner that holds up to 480 newborn and 220 large diapers and can be cleaned with bleach.

t he hours you spend in the nursery feeding and rocking baby to sleep will be among the most pleasant and peaceful of her early months—most of the time. You might as well spend these hours in comfort in a nursery chair of some kind.

After all the other expenses of baby's room are tallied, an investment in a special nursery chair may seem excessive; but what seems like a luxury now will be a necessity as late-night feedings become a way of life. The nursery should feel as warm, welcoming, and comfortable for you as it does for your baby; after all, it will be your home, too, for the first year or so. So invest in a good rocker or glider, both of which produce the gentle rocking motion that babies love, or consider such alternatives as a chaise, a standard armchair with a footstool, or a day bed.

If you'll be shopping for a new piece of furniture, look for sturdiness and comfort. Check the frame, and sit in the chair to be sure it suits you. Remember it should be comfortable for both parents, and for long periods of time. Prefer going the vintage route? Porch rockers made of wood or wicker can be cleaned up, painted, and complemented with charming seat cushions. But check them carefully for signs of wear, protruding nails, splintery wood, and anything else that could harm baby.

chairs and mobiles

Rockers are a time-honored choice, but some models have a tendency to move across the floor as you rock; you may want to invest a little money in a model that stays put.

Rocker/gliders are widely available in a great many styles, finishes, and upholstery choices; and some offer a ball-bearing mechanism that lets you rock for long periods of time with no inching forward and very little strain on the back. Some people prefer armchairs, even though there's no built-in rocking motion; but for those who like rocking, some newer arm chairs are being equipped with rockers.

Keep in mind that you don't necessarily need to match your nursery chair to the decor of baby's room; instead, blend it with the look of the master bedroom or family room, where you might move it later.

ABOVE This nursery chair is designed with an extra-wide seat for more comfortable nursing. Later, it will fit both you and a toddler for sharing a storybook.

RIGHT You can rock baby to sleep in a portable bassinet, such as this simple, sophisticated style.

OPPOSITE Ready for a late-night feeding, this armchair offers a footstool in matching fabric, a pillow, and a soft blanket.

easy clean

Splurge a little on a luxury that will save you time and effort in the long run—a wipe-clean finish for the cushions or upholstery of your nursery chair.

RIGHT No matter what style you choose for your nursery chair, try to place it close to the crib so that you can quickly put baby back to bed once you have lulled her to sleep.

BELOW In this cushy chair you and your baby can rock or just recline.

BELOW RIGHT Fans of contemporary design will love this bold armchair.

a comfy chair makes time together more cozy

RIGHT A chenille slipcover makes this armchair cozy and comfortable. When it's soiled, just toss it in the washing machine.

BELOW RIGHT This Intriguing piece mixes rocker legs with classic wing-chair styling.

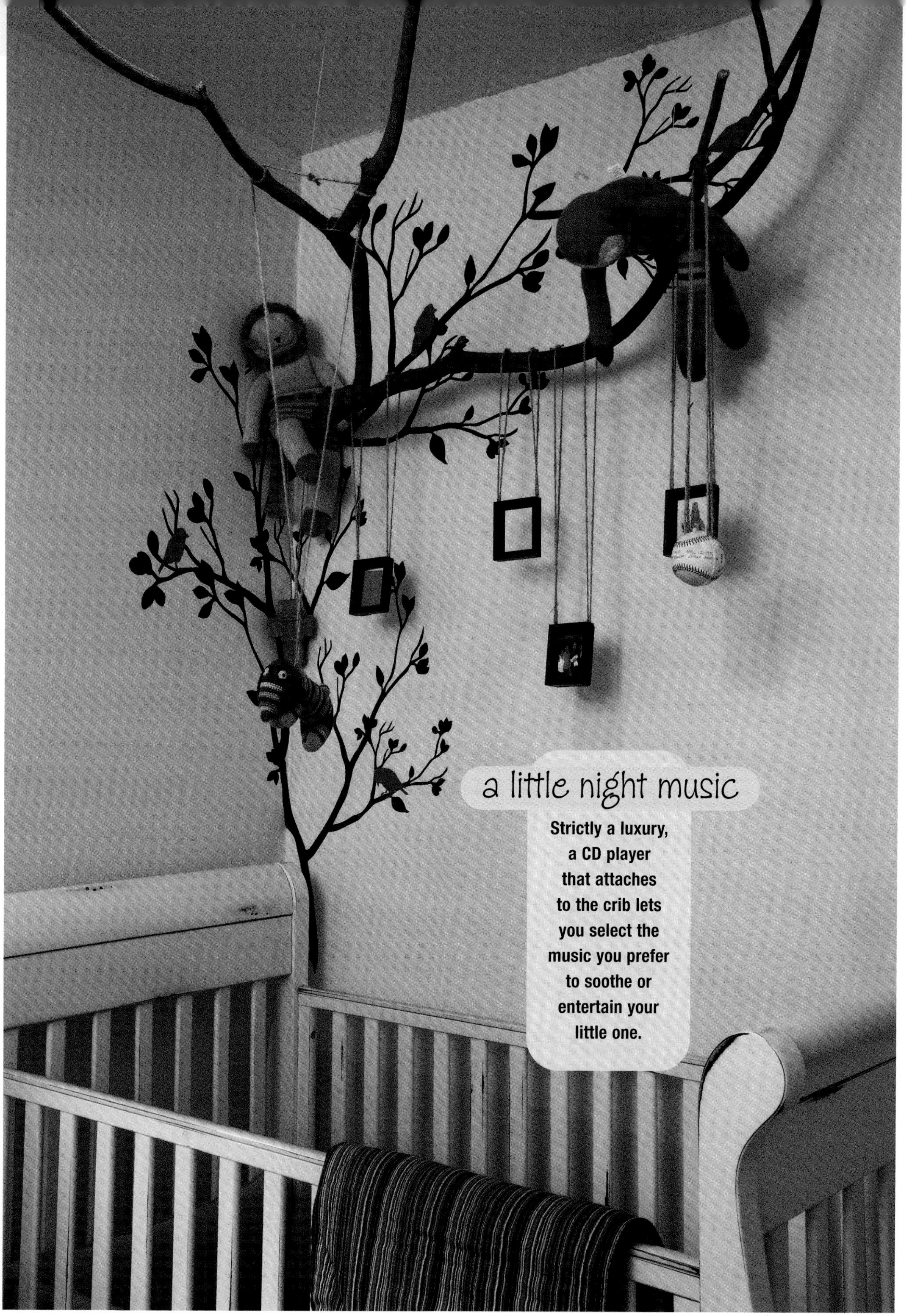

a little night music

Strictly a luxury,
a CD player
that attaches
to the crib lets
you select the
music you prefer
to soothe or
entertain your
little one.

mobiles

A mobile, particularly a colorful one that plays music, will entertain baby and stimulate his eye-tracking and sound-perception skills. You can play a musical mobile to lull your infant to sleep or wind up the music box to encourage play. Some music boxes operate by remote control, a feature that will come in handy in case baby begins to cry when the music ends. A mobile may come with more than one musical selection and offer different types of movement and motion to stimulate developing senses.

Most mobiles are easy to assemble, contain washable parts, and come with an attachment mechanism that fits most cribs. Some models can also be adapted to fit strollers and car seats.

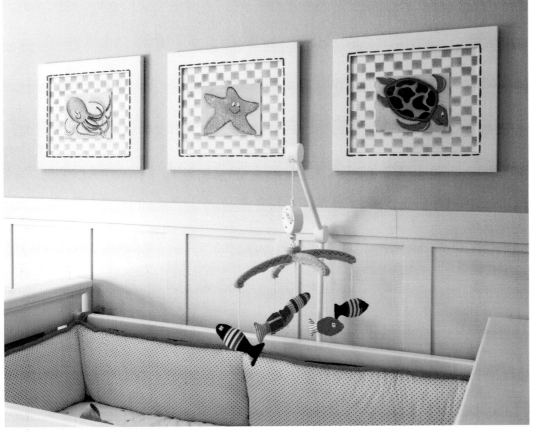

OPPOSITE Part mural, part real, this nursery tree is full of interesting things for baby to see.

ABOVE Musical mobiles stimulate both eyes and ears, paying big dividends in baby development.

LEFT Here, the mobile matches both the color and the nautical theme in the nursery.

6

Toddlers' Rooms

As your child evolves from a newborn to an increasingly independent tot, he will form an attachment to his room and see it as an extension of himself. So it is important to plan a room that not only pleases his senses but serves his needs. In this time of transition, your toddler will move from a crib to a bed, acquire special belongings, and develop his motor and language skills. As you decorate, you'll be making important choices—buying a bed, planning areas for play, creating storage, and making the room safe for all activities.

- **the first steps**
- **creating a design plan**
- **furniture and lighting**
- **storage**
- **kids' baths**

This toddler's room features a child-size chair and a very grown-up bed.

t he change from nursery to "big-kid's room" may be somewhat disruptive for a toddler despite her increasing sense of independence. There are a number of things you can do to prepare your child for a smooth transition. First—and perhaps most important—communicate with her. It's never too soon to start talking about upcoming changes. Emphasize that because your child is not a baby anymore, she is going to sleep in a grown-up bed and have "big-girl" furniture. Whether there will be a move to a new room or not, explain that the new space will belong to her. Parents of preschoolers hear the word "mine" often enough to know that the concept of ownership is very appealing.

Secondly, involve your child in the process. Let him "help" you by taking some of his things from the nursery into his new room. If you're reorganizing the nursery, show him where his things will now be kept and ask him to put some of them away. You can also ask your toddler to help choose the design of the room. After all, it's going to be the child's special place, and he should have the right—within reason—to have a say in how it's going to look.

the first steps

TOP LEFT A favorite mural helps make a toddler feel right at home.

TOP RIGHT Who says the door to a kid's room must be conventional? This kid-size Dutch door is great for imaginary play.

RIGHT AND OPPOSITE These two rooms feature a beach theme, which the occupants enjoy all year long.

a room built for play

Room to play is probably the most important thing you can provide for your toddler. Kids of this age need activity—a rocking horse, indoor gym set, big blocks, and other large items. If space permits, divide the room into separate areas for sleep, storytelling, crafts, and active play. You may be able to contain some of the mess by permitting finger painting, say, only at the crafts table and restricting toys to the play area. You can visually partition the space by positioning furniture strategically. Make sure you don't incorporate items that are easy to tip over, and be sure to use nonskid area rugs to designate different zones.

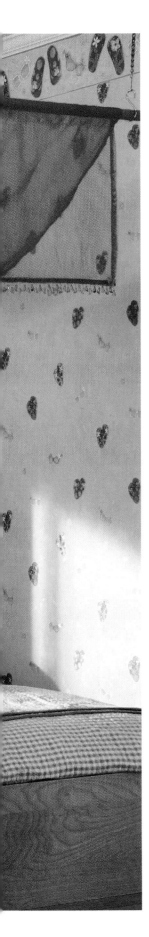

c reating a decorative scheme for your toddler's room will be an easy task if you are simply updating the nursery into a little kid's room. While babyish themes will become inappropriate by the end of the toddler years, some storybook characters or simple floral designs may be acceptable all the way through elementary school. However, if you're starting from scratch, you've got a little more work ahead.

The best place to begin is with color. Color is an excellent way to get your child excited about a new room. You can easily and economically update a nursery with new window treatments, wallpaper borders, or a couple of nonskid scatter rugs in bright shades. Although your toddler's color preferences may change overnight, recent studies do indicate that bright colors are very appealing at this age, and red and yellow appear to be particular favorites. In general, bright colors are psychologically stimulating while cool colors have a relaxing affect.

If you—or your child—dislike bright or primary colors, choose a neutral overall scheme and accent it with bright shades of red, blue, yellow, or, perhaps, a combination of these hues. Many of the toys and accessories designed for children of this age are decorated in bright colors, which makes accessorizing the room that much easier.

You can also create a monochromatic scheme by experimenting with various tints and shades of one primary color. For example, try using different shades of blue for the walls, trim, window treatments, comforter, sheets, and throw pillows. If your child gets tired of the scheme, just change the color of one of these elements.

Should you decide to invest in more significant changes, go with something that will grow with your child, such as geometric prints, stripes, plaids, or any other classic motif. Design choices such as these will last well into the school years, or at least until your child—or you—grows tired of them.

creating a design plan

A new bed, a matching chest, and some cheery wallpaper can transform the nursery into a toddler's room with a minimum of fuss and expense.

essential furnishings

Build your room design around these basics. While you don't have to buy everything on this list, it will serve as a guideline for planning your budget.

- Bed
- Chest of drawers
- Toy box
- Nightstand
- Lighting
- Small table and chairs
- Flooring

Go Green

Look for wood furniture with a Forest Stewardship Council (FSC) label, proof that the wood was recycled or responsibly harvested.

OPPOSITE TOP Older children might enjoy helping to choose wallpaper patterns and bedding for their own rooms.

OPPOSITE BOTTOM Custom-designed bunk beds are great for sleepovers; storage drawers underneath the bottom bunk are a bonus.

RIGHT Make sure your toddler's first bed is sturdy and wide enough to hold him securely.

furniture and lighting

Choose fun furnishings and lighting to personalize your child's room, but resist the urge to go overboard. One dresser is probably sufficient for a toddler. But hold off on the mirror for that dresser, or put it in storage for a while. Toys and objects tend to fly around the room when young children play, and a large mirror that can shatter is a potential hazard.

If you plan to add more than just a bed and a single dresser, choose clean-line designs that work with a variety of decorating styles. Check that furniture and lamps have met the standards of the Juvenile Products Manufacturers Association (JPMA) and the Consumer Products Safety Commission (CPSC).

what kind of bed?

A twin-size adult bed is an ideal choice for a toddler's room. If you've got the space, buy two twins now. As your child gets older, she'll want to invite friends for sleepovers. Some twin beds have removable guardrails, a must for a toddler who is adjusting to a grown-up bed.

Toddler beds are generally smaller and lower to the floor than standard-size beds. They do not have guardrails and seldom feature box springs, which means there is not enough support for a growing body. Shop for a twin mattress with at least 200 coils; 300 coils if you are buying a double bed. A headboard and footboard are optional and can be added later.

play space

A platform built into a corner of your child's room creates visual interest and provides a special nook for reading, board games, and even a show.

OPPOSITE TOP This little girl's room features a raised area for reading, playing, and daydreaming.

OPPOSITE BOTTOM Being able to sleep in a grown-up bed is an important milestone in a child's life.

LEFT Furnish your kid's room with colors and accessories that reflect his budding interests.

BELOW Many kids would be thrilled with the idea of sleeping in a race car. Keep in mind, though, that not all novelty beds are constructed for extended use.

novelty beds

Beds shaped like racing cars, trucks, or castles usually retain their appeal for kids until age 8 or 10. After that, they may be passed down to another child.

C is for car

S is for scooter

T is for tricycle

W is for wagon

BELOW A pretty curtain adds a little glamour and effectively divides this room into a nursery and a private sleeping space for an older child.

OPPOSITE Bunk beds can be an ideal solution to the two-kids-in-one-bedroom challenge, and they can be great space savers. Here, there's plenty of floor space for a play section and a sitting area for quiet activities.

sharing a room

It's not unusual for two young children to share a room; and if they're close to the same age, it usually works out well. Each child should have his own bed and, ideally, separate storage for toys and clothes. The play space and activity table can usually be shared successfully.

Of course, a school-age child is not always thrilled to share a room with a younger sibling. To keep the peace, divide the room into private areas using furniture or a movable screen to demarcate the sections. For safety and privacy, provide storage for the older child that the younger one cannot reach.

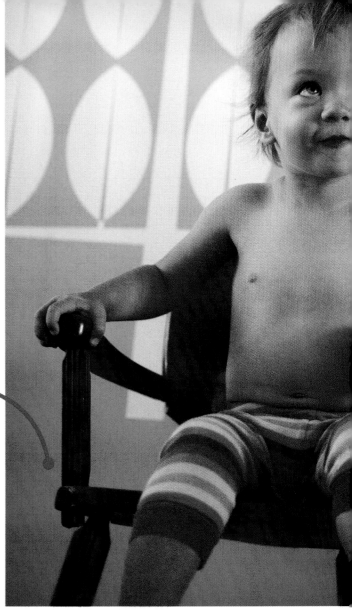

confidence booster

Experts say that using a table and chair tailored perfectly for a little body gives a child a boost of confidence, pride, and self-esteem.

OPPOSITE TOP Fuzzy friends are treated to a tea party at this charming table set, hand-painted to match the custom floorcloth.

LEFT Children are thrilled when they have furniture of their own.

OPPOSITE BOTTOM If you like keeping an eye on the kids while they play, set up a table and chairs just for them in the family room or a corner of the kitchen.

BOTTOM LEFT AND BELOW Consider buying prefinished furniture or applying a protective coat to make the top of a toddler table easy to keep clean. Make sure you choose a nontoxic product.

cleanability

If you're going to paint any of the furniture in your toddler's room, use a semigloss paint finish, which may be wiped clean with a damp sponge.

table and chairs

A tot-size table-and-chair set provides a place for fantasy and creativity. Little ones like to get their fingers into things, and this is the spot where they can indulge that desire and safely play with such messy things as paints, crayons, and clay. A table and chairs also allow for imaginary events such as grown-up tea parties with teddy bears or other little ones. And of course, it's a good place for real snacks, too.

Pint-size tables and chairs are widely available. You can buy a prefinished wood set that matches the furniture in the room or opt for unfinished wood, which you can paint whatever color you like. Plastic is another option—a sturdy plastic set can take a real beating, and you can scrub it without ruining the finish.

for story time, place a reading lamp next to the bed

lighting for little ones

As you furnish your toddler's room, give some thought to lighting. At this stage, effective overall illumination is a necessity. So, too, is a soft, unobtrusive night-light you can leave on for the times that you may need to check on your little one. Fears about the dark begin to emerge during these years, so a night-light will be comforting to your toddler, as well. For storybook time, you'll also need a reading light placed near the bed, next to a comfortable chair, or wherever you will sit while reading to your child. Task lighting is not a requirement for children of this age—their short attention spans preclude long-term concentration on one task.

For effective overall illumination, opt for recessed or ceiling-mounted fixtures installed on a dimmer switch. Avoid table lamps, as they can fall over and their cords can trip rambunctious children. Instead, use a wall-mounted fixture with a light source you can direct.

OPPOSITE Coordinated with the bed linens and wallcovering, this table lamp is a great addition to a girl's room.

LEFT When they finally have rooms of their own, kids love having fun objects around them. Each of the lamps shown here would work well on a dresser or desk, provided the cord is tucked safely out of reach.

ABOVE Installing a jaunty chandelier like this one is a good way to light up a child's room. She'll enjoy its colorful design, and it will provide the bright overall illumination necessary for play and reading.

it's hard to believe that a child who's been in the world for only two or three years can own enough stuff to require a storage system. But as all parents know, children's things accumulate quickly; and they need to be dealt with before chaos overcomes the room.

What's most important is a storage system for the many toys that your toddler has accumulated. Crates, cubbies, and plastic bins are excellent solutions. Bins on wheels are especially handy at the end of the day when it's time to pick up toys scattered across the room. A traditional toy box is useful, too, as long as it features safety hinges. Vintage trunks make interesting toy boxes, but they, too, must be retrofitted with safety hinges. Whatever you choose, you must find a place to put toys. A child getting out of bed at night can easily trip over items left on the floor.

storage

Shelves are another good idea. If your child is a climber, a set of open shelves will be an invitation to explore, and could be dangerous. But if the shelves are low enough for him to reach easily, they will help him learn to pick up after himself. Adjustable shelves that fit on sturdy, wall-mounted brackets offer the most flexibility. Another handy idea—affix the bottoms of plastic crates to the wall so they can serve as storage cubbies. Anything heavy, such as high bookcases or other tall storage pieces, should be bolted to the wall as well.

For bulkier items, install a closet organizer. Easy-to-assemble wire-coated systems come in numerous configurations and include bins, baskets, drawers, and shelves. Lower hanging rods make it possible for kids to hang up their own clothes; kid-height clothes trees and pegged racks are also useful for this purpose.

OPPOSITE Low shelves fitted with baskets keep toys, books, and other large items within easy reach.

LEFT These hand-painted storage bins will help your little one learn the alphabet in no time.

ABOVE This cushioned bench doubles as a low bookcase.

BELOW Your child can use this sleek storage unit for many years.

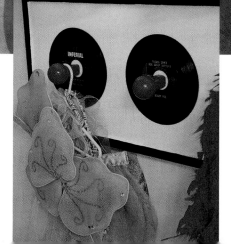

ABOVE Bolted to the wall for safety, these locker-type storage units hold clothes, toys, and books. Seasonal and seldom-used items are stored on a high shelf.

RIGHT Because standard hangers are difficult for toddlers to use properly, hooks and pegs will help instill tidy habits at an early age.

RIGHT A handy homeowner could easily build a shelving system, such as this one, using inexpensive, readily available materials.

BELOW This custom-designed toddler room features loads of built-in storage for clothes, books, and toys.

custom-built storage

One way to provide toddler storage is to have something built to your exact specifications. If it's in your budget, this can be a wise investment—particularly in a small room with little space for furniture—and it will probably serve your child's needs for years to come. If you hire a professional carpenter, explain that you expect the pieces to accommodate your child's storage needs now (stuffed animals, toys, storybooks) and in the future (heavy textbooks or perhaps a TV). Don't forget to get references and check them carefully; then obtain several estimates for the work.

organize kid stuff with built-ins, cubbies, and shelves

ABOVE A kid-friendly wall rack stores books, games, and toys, keeping them organized and in plain sight.

LEFT Toy chests fitted with safety hinges are handy for quick and easy storage. Topped with a soft cushion, this one doubles as seating.

OPPOSITE This hand-painted armoire is sure to delight your little girl for many years to come.

the right height

To prevent possible injuries to kids' eyes, mount pegboard-style storage at least 36 in. above the floor.

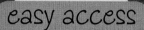

easy access

Cupboards
with doors keep
clutter out of
sight, but they
also prevent a
child from finding
toys quickly and
putting them
away easily.
Open shelves
and cubbies
are better.

OPPOSITE FAR LEFT To create a cohesive design scheme, choose freestanding storage pieces that match other colors in the room.

OPPOSITE TOP Used now for toys, this little rolling shelf unit can be filled with books when your child is older.

OPPOSITE BOTTOM Utilize every inch of available space for storage. These easy-glide drawers, built into a window seat, are ideal for keeping seldom-used toys out of sight.

ABOVE The open shelves in this room are just the right height for a toddler to reach to find a favorite puzzle, book, or toy.

kids' baths

most children share a bath with the rest of the family. A lucky few have their own bathrooms. If that's the case in your household, you can have some fun decorating the bath to please your child. Keep in mind that safety is the most important design feature. (For more on bathroom safety for kids, see Chapter 7.)

Most bathrooms are small and don't need much in the way of decorating. To start, select a neutral shade for the toilet, tub, sinks, and vanity cabinets. This strategy will make choosing decorative elements easier and will prevent the room from looking dated too quickly. Then add a bit of color and some whimsical touches to appeal to your child's sense of fun. Young children like bright color, but resist the temptation to go overboard. A vivid shade of paint on the walls or brightly colored tiles will harmonize with a theme-driven shower curtain and matching border. But if you bring in too many different patterns—in the wallcovering and towels and window treatments, for example—the room will look busy. And after a while, this kind of design chaos will make it less appealing, too. Another approach is to keep the walls and floor neutral, too, and let the accessories you choose provide all the color and decorative interest. This way, you can update the look every few years—or more often, if you like—without spending a lot.

Unless you have several young children—or plan to have them—it's not economical to install child-height sinks and toilets. Instead, use sturdy stools that give kids the temporary boost they need.

The private domain of a lucky little girl, this bath is filled with enchanting features—a dressing table, a vibrant color scheme, and a large tub. The dressing table is a flea-market find treated to a fresh coat of paint.

Go Green

As an alternative to mildew removers that contain toxic chemicals, try white vinegar. Studies show that it kills 99 percent of bacteria and 82 percent of mold.

sharing a bath

If two children are using the same bath, establishing as much equality as possible will make sharing a more peaceful experience. If there is space, install dual sinks, vanity cabinets, and mirrors, which will give each child a sense of ownership. If there's no space for dual equipment—or the budget doesn't allow for it—personalized robes, towels, and hooks for each child can have the same effect. These efforts will do more than keep the peace—in a kid-friendly bath, your child will be less likely to resist brushing her teeth or toilet training.

add color and whimsy to your child's bath

OPPOSITE TOP A toddler may need a leg up at the sink to brush his teeth and wash his face. Buy or build a sturdy stool to help him.

OPPOSITE BOTTOM A fun and appealing bath design might make your child actually look forward to brushing his teeth.

ABOVE To reduce tidying-up time, choose quick-clean surfaces and fabrics.

LEFT The fish on the shower curtain and the colors of the towels coordinate beautifully with the wallcovering in this bath.

Keeping Them Safe

It's no surprise that most parents worry about the health and well-being of their little ones. To a new parent, even innocent-seeming items—a fluffy blanket, a penny, a small toy—seem fraught with potential danger. While there's no need to panic, keeping baby safe does require a careful assessment not just of the nursery but—as your child becomes more mobile—every area of your home.

- the nursery
- the toddler's room
- the bathroom

To protect your little one from harm, assess the safety of every room in your home—especially his bedroom and bathroom—and make them childproof.

there are a few caveats about keeping your infant safe in the nursery that bear repeating. First, choose a bassinet or cradle with a sturdy bottom and a wide base. Inspect hand-me-downs or flea-market finds carefully, checking interior and exterior surfaces for splinters, staples, protruding nails, or other potential sources of injury. Do the cradle's legs fold? If so, inspect the leg locks—you don't want them to collapse when the bassinet or cradle is in use. A safety strap for a changing table is also a good idea. If necessary, buy a safety strap and attach it yourself—and always use it to keep baby from wriggling off the table.

You'll need to consider a number of other issues regarding products sold for babies and toddlers. Spend some time browsing Web sites, such as those of the Juvenile Products Manufacturers Association (JPMA), the National Safety Council (NSC), and WebMD, all of which offer detailed information on safety practices, product standards, and tips for making the entire home child safe. Check the Resource Guide beginning on page 192 for more information on these and other organizations.

the nursery

One of the most important steps you can take to protect baby—and your whole family—is to install at least one smoke detector on every level of your house. A large, multilevel house may require more than one unit per floor. If you heat your home with oil or gas or have an attached garage, place carbon-monoxide detectors near all of the bedrooms. Change the batteries in all of these devices according to manufacturers' recommendations, or at least once a year. Contact your local building department for the latest information on how to keep your smoke detectors in prime working condition.

safety in the nursery

Here are some safety tips for furnishing baby's first room.

- **Bedding**. Put baby on his back to sleep; avoid soft bedding that might suffocate him. Crib slats should be 2⅜ inches apart or less so his head can't get trapped.
- **Changing table.** Use a sturdy table with 2-inch guardrails on all sides. Always use a safety strap; keep diapering supplies within easy reach.
- **Crib toys.** Remove mobiles and gyms when baby is 5 months old or can push up on hands and knees.
- **Window cords.** Never place a crib near windows; cut looped chains or blind cords in half to avoid strangulation.
- **Toy chests.** Use chests without lids or with safety hinges that prevent the lid from closing on little hands.
- **Balls, balloons, other small toys.** Keep them away from the crib to avoid a potential choking hazard.

Get a head start on safety by making sure baby's first furniture is accident-proof. Choose a crib with up-to-date safety features; provide plenty of fresh air; and remove soft pillows, stuffed toys, and bedding when it's time for baby to sleep.

crib toy safety

Follow these tips from the Juvenile Product Safety Association (JPSA) for choosing items that are safe for baby's crib.

- Take rattles, squeeze toys, teethers, plush toys, and other items out of baby's crib when he is asleep or unattended.
- Strings can cause strangulation! Never string a pacifier or any other item around baby's neck.
- Remove crib gyms and mobiles from the crib when baby begins to push up on hands and knees.
- Mobiles and any other toys that hang over the crib should be positioned out of reach.

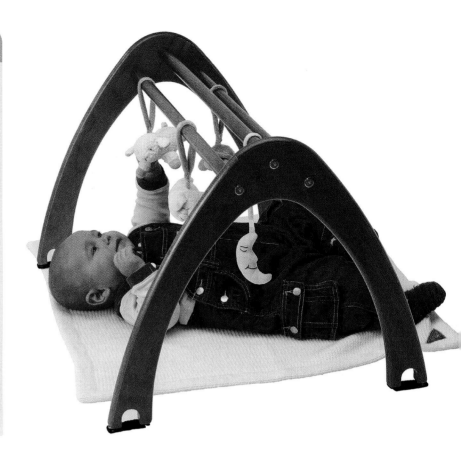

breathable bumpers

Many pediatricians now recommend replacing traditional padded bumpers with mesh crib liners that protect baby from injury or suffocation.

ABOVE Mobiles encourage physical and mental development, but be sure to keep small items that could be swallowed away from babies.

LEFT Well-made, sturdy toys can provide hours of safe fun and entertainment.

OPPOSITE Make sure that decorative padded crib bumpers are tied snugly in place when it's time for baby to sleep.

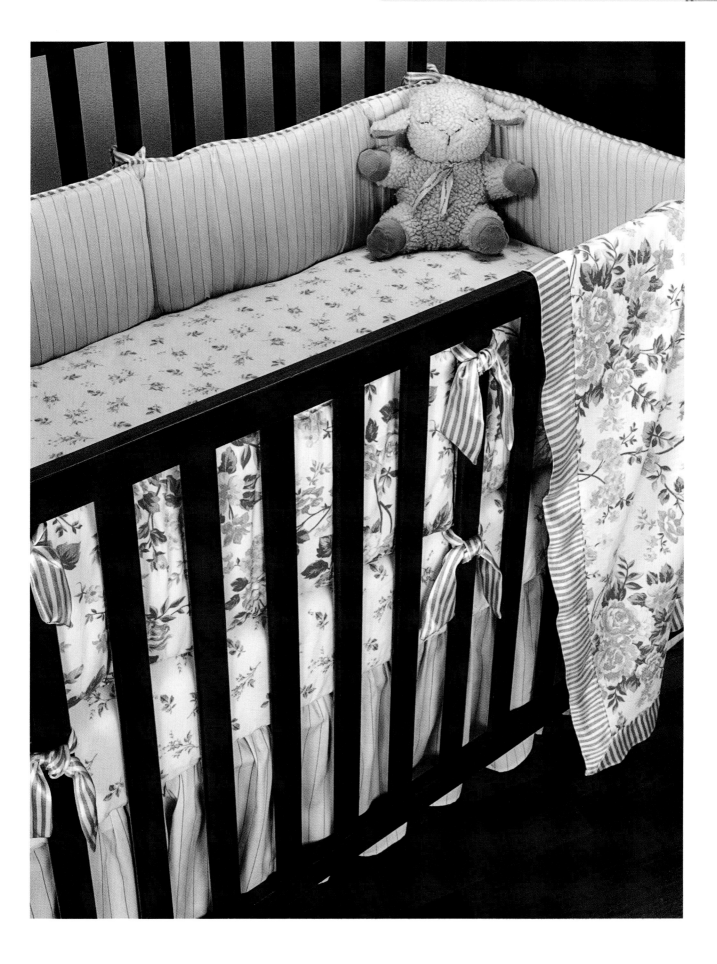

ABOVE Crib heights are generally for the parents' comfort, but for baby's safety, you might consider one that sits closer to the floor.

RIGHT The changing table in this nursery boasts a comfortable pad and side rails to keep your infant from falling.

BELOW From the security of a crib that meets all safety standards, this baby can enjoy—and learn basic skills from—a sweet wall appliqué that tells a story.

make sure baby's

crib notes

Use bumper pads only until your child can pull up to a standing position. Then remove them so baby cannot use the pads to climb out of the crib.

first furniture has smooth, rounded edges

you'll rest easier knowing

the toddler's room

With their natural curiosity and fast-growing independence, toddlers seem to be drawn like magnets to potential sources of harm. In addition to bolting tippable furniture to the wall in the nursery or toddler's room, take this precaution with any tall piece that a tenacious climbing child could dislodge elsewhere in the house. Also block electrical outlets and power cords in all rooms with childproof plastic caps.

You might want to keep pets out of baby's bed with a crib tent, which will also help prevent her from climbing or falling. These mesh domes are secured to the crib or bed rails with hook-and-loop tape.

LEFT Sleeping in her first grown-up bed is a great thrill for a child. Recycle an older child's bed with a new coat of paint in a color of her choice, and she will feel like it's her own. Table lamps—not a good idea for toddlers—are fine for an older child.

BELOW A tot-size armchair is a charming and useful addition to a child's bedroom.

toddler safety tips

Take these steps to childproof your toddler's room.

- Remove table lamps or secure them with industrial-strength hook-and-loop tape.
- Install slide locks to prevent toddlers from opening and closing bifold doors that can catch fingers. Install the locks so that they are out of reach.
- Keep conventional doors from closing or accidentally slamming shut by using foam doorstops that fit over the top of the door.
- Do not install a lock on the door.

LEFT Consider buying a crib that will convert to a toddler bed when your child is ready.

BELOW Gates can keep both babies and pets from getting into trouble. Tall ones are the most useful.

OPPOSITE To prevent the possibility of heavy furniture tipping over onto a small child, choose pieces that are sturdy and low to the ground.

childproofing the home

Here are a few suggestions for preventing accidents throughout the house.

- Use safety gates at the top and bottom of stairs and in the doorways of rooms you don't want your toddler to enter. Gates with expanding pressure bars should be placed facing away from baby.
- Use doorknob covers to keep children out of rooms and other areas with hazards, such as swimming pools. Be careful, though, that these devices are easy for adults to use in case of emergency.
- Put corner and edge bumpers on furniture and other items, such as fireplace hearths, to protect against injury.
- Place furniture away from high windows so children won't climb onto windowsills. Screens aren't strong enough to keep children from falling through a window.
- Make sure window blinds do not have looped cords—these can be a strangulation hazard for children. Blinds, shades, and draperies purchased before 2001 should be updated or replaced. Also, always lock blinds into position whether they are all the way up or down.
- Remove free-falling lids from toy chests, which should have a lid that is secured with safety latches or a light, removable cover.
- Prevent furniture from tipping by securing bookcases, shelving, and heavy furniture to walls using brackets and anchors.

watch the wicker

Wicker baskets and other decorative items wear out over time. Watch for small pieces that may break off and present a choking hazard.

the bathroom

t he first safety rule of the bathroom is to supervise young children in the tub at absolutely all times. The second rule: no matter how vigilant your supervision, childproof the room anyway. Install grab bars and antiscald faucets in the tub, and cover the bottom with a nonskid mat. At bath time, fill the tub only high enough to cover baby's legs. Use a bath seat or ring, making sure the suction cups that attach it to the tub are securely fastened. Keep the toilet lid down, and use a toilet latch. Remember that babies can drown in only a few inches of water.

Elsewhere in the room, cover all electrical outlets and unplug appliances when not in use. Store medicines and cleaning products in locked cabinets, on high shelves, or in another room.

Floors in the bath routinely get wet. Protect little ones from slipping and falling by choosing textured vinyl or tiles as a floor covering, or put down area rugs with nonslip backings.

FAR LEFT Patterns and colors with kid appeal enliven this bath. The plush rug has a skidproof backing.

LEFT Here's the perfect tub accessory—a fun frog caddy that holds bath-time necessities, including a rubber duck.

BELOW This molded-plastic baby bath is a safe and handy alternative to the family tub.

water safety

Install antiscalding devices on faucets and showerheads to prevent burns. Also set the water heater no higher than 120 degrees.

LEFT A built-in laundry hamper is a nifty bathroom feature.

BELOW Install safety latches on any cabinets that store potentially hazardous items.

RIGHT Pullout steps give little ones the height they need to reach the sink in this kids' bath.

pay close attention to the drawers and cabinets in

bathroom cabinets

Toddlers are notorious for getting into everything. In the bathroom, especially, an ounce of prevention is worth a pound of cure.

- Always label medicines carefully. This can be useful for kids old enough to read and also as a preventive measure against accidentally administering the wrong medicine to a child.
- Always use childproof caps.
- Install safety latches or locks on cabinets and drawers to keep children from potentially poisonous household products.
- Discourage children from putting anything except food in their mouths.

safety proof

Return all medicine products to locked storage immediately, and keep the products and your children in sight during use.

the rooms your children use

8

Health and Special Needs

I f your child has medical or physical challenges, you may have to adapt the nursery to meet their special requirements. By making some thoughtful modifications—and by choosing green, eco-friendly products whenever possible—the nursery can be safe, stimulating, and appropriately designed for whatever challenges your son or daughter may face. Your efforts now will help your child well into her school-age years. What's more, many of these modifications will also benefit the rest of the family.

- **accommodating disabilities**
- **addressing allergies**
- **keeping it green**

Nontoxic materials, natural light, and fresh air help make a room healthful for your child.

accommodating disabilities

Some children face physical challenges, such as visual, hearing, or mobility issues, which must be considered when you are planning and designing their bedroom. If your child is visually impaired, for example, you need to provide bright light, which is beneficial, but prevent glare, which is not. Choose furniture with matte finishes and be cautious about reflective surfaces. Because natural light is more helpful than artificial light, try to locate the nursery in a room that gets plenty of natural light but not too much direct sunshine. A southeastern exposure on one wall will provide more than enough natural illumination. When decorating, choose accessories, toys, and fabrics with bright contrast to give baby the visual interest and stimulation he needs.

If your child has a physical disability, you'll want to anticipate and reassess his needs and abilities and make modifications to his room design as he grows. Issues to consider include both his fine and gross motor skills, upper-body strength, extent of reach, and stamina. Will an injury or disability require your child to use a wheelchair or walker in the future? If so, you'll need to make changes in the size of the room or the width of the doorways. To turn around, a wheelchair requires a circular area that is 5 feet in diameter; door openings must be at least 32 inches wide to allow a wheelchair to move through. If the nursery is too small to meet these space requirements, you may need to move the baby to another room in the future or borrow space from an adjoining room to enlarge the nursery. You can make the doorway more accessible by installing a pocket door or by adding offset or swing-clear hinges to the existing door. If those fixes don't solve the problem, you may have to call in a contractor to widen the opening.

If your child will have difficulty gripping and turning knobs, replace them with lever- or loop-style hardware. These are available in two types—one that installs permanently, and one that the child can take with her to use on any door in the house. A good way to determine door accessibility is the closed-fist test. If you can't open the door with one hand closed into a fist, you will need to make an adaptation.

RIGHT This black and white activity mat provides plenty of visual stimulation.

FAR RIGHT Matte surfaces and boldly contrasting colors make this nursery ideal for a baby with a visual impairment.

smart solutions to special challenges

Leslie Saul, founder of Leslie Saul & Associates, an architecture and design firm in Cambridge, Massachusetts, has provided design solutions for many families with special needs. As baby gets older and becomes increasingly mobile, she'll need a room that provides her with safety, comfort, and—equally important—a sense of independence. Saul offers these guidelines for designing a room to meet the growing needs of a disabled child.

For a child with a visual impairment, sound takes on heightened importance, Saul says. Recognizing the different sounds that bounce off various surfaces (wood floors versus carpeted ones, for example) helps the child to navigate the space. To enhance these auditory cues, she recommends varying the textures in your child's room. For example,

- Upholster a wall and install carpeting near the bed for a cozy area, but leave the floors and walls uncovered in a play space.
- To signal the entrance to the child's room, consider adding a motion detector connected to a digital recorder that plays a special greeting or her favorite tune.
- Make sure carpeting is flush with hardwood floors to avoid tripping.
- Install a chair rail your child can use as a comfortable guide around the perimeter of the room.
- Organize toys in simple bins and drawers. Use knobs or pulls in different shapes on drawers and closets to help identify their contents.

For a child in a wheelchair, the wall treatments can be anything you prefer. However, it's important to keep floor surfaces flush with one another, whether carpeted or hardwood, says Saul.

- Carpets should have a tight weave to allow for maximum mobility.
- Extra space around all of the furniture is necessary; you can maximize this by installing a wall-mounted desk and drawers.
- Use extra-heavy-duty drawer slides with a self-closing mechanism. These require a minimal effort to open and only a light touch to close.
- Add a chair rail or handrail for extra assistance around the perimeter of the room.

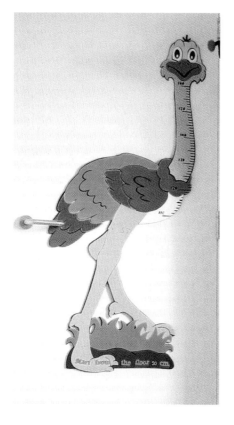

OPPOSITE Designed for a child with physical challenges, this room features a lower bunk that's easy to reach and a desk that can accommodate a wheelchair.

LEFT A colorful mural on the door will help a visually impaired child identify her room. The lever-style door handle is easy to use.

more helpful ideas

Here are some additional steps you can take to improve the functionality of your child's room and enhance his independence:

- **Maximize areas of ability.** A child who has a lower-extremity disability, for example, may have no problems with activities that call upon upper-body strength. In this case, you may not want to eliminate furniture with drawers or remove closet doors, because opening them allows him to use these unaffected muscle groups.
- **Seek advice.** Nonprofit organizations devoted to various medical conditions can be excellent resources. Many encourage parent communication and support that you'll get nowhere else. Most of these groups have Web sites that are easily located through a quick Internet search.

less is more

In the nursery, the fewer the furnishings, surfaces, and fabrics that collect allergens, the healthier the environment will be.

addressing allergies

A simply furnished and decorated child's room, such as this one, is free of the frills that often attract dust and air pollutants.

babies who have been diagnosed with asthma or environmental allergies need a place to play and sleep that is as free as possible from triggering agents. Typically these agents, known as allergens, include dust mites, animal dander, certain types of plants, some insects, mold, fungi, and fabric fragments. If your baby or toddler is diagnosed with allergies or asthma, there are several things you can do to create a healthful environment in the nursery.

The first line of defense is to get rid of dust and other allergens as thoroughly as possible. This means more than vacuuming regularly—it also means not providing a home for them in the first place. Dust collects readily in the pleats and folds of curtain fabric, upholstered and slipcovered furniture, and frilly lampshades—so keep fabric accessories to a minimum. Also eliminate other places where dust could settle. For example, dusting a roller blind is easy and fast, but a miniblind, with its many small slats, takes time and may stir up more dust. Another drawback to this type of window treatment is that on a busy day you may tempted to skip dusting it altogether. Special bedding such as allergen-free mattress covers and linens designed for asthmatic children may also help.

Plush toys are another potential source of allergens. To be on the safe side—and with the approval of your pediatrician or family doctor—limit the baby's supply to one or two washable stuffed animals; then be sure to clean them regularly. Eliminating dust will greatly improve air quality for your child. Maximize this effect by conditioning the air so that it is not hot and humid but slightly on the dry side. This will help children with asthma and allergies breathe easier. Install an air conditioner and start using it in early spring at the beginning of the allergy season. The ideal relative humidity is 30 to 50 percent. However, if you live in an area where the humidity rises to levels that your air conditioner cannot handle you may also need to use a dehumidifier. For children with severe allergies, a high-efficiency particulate air (HEPA) filter may be helpful. Talk to your doctor about the baby's specific needs regarding air filtration and humidity control.

wash bed linens in hot water

twice weekly to eliminate allergens

OPPOSITE For the bath, where mold can be a problem, choose moisture-resistant fabrics and launder them often.

ABOVE If your child has allergies, avoid carpeting in her room. Area rugs are fine if they are machine-washable.

RIGHT The sleeker the furniture, the less chance that it will harbor dust and other allergens.

win the war against troublesome allergens

While you're waging the battle against allergens, you might as well get rid of as many as you possibly can, including pet dander, cigarette smoke, and mold.

Even if your child tolerates the family pet, keep contact confined to the general living areas of the house. Be firm about keeping pets out of the nursery. Because pet dander, urine, or saliva may trigger an attack, you should also keep Fido or Felix from climbing on upholstered furniture, lying on carpets or rugs, or rolling around on clean piles of laundry.

An asthmatic child can have an attack simply from being exposed to smoke from a cigarette, cigar, or pipe, or from the smoke exhaled by someone using those tobacco products. Never allow anyone to smoke in your house or your car.

Mold, which thrives in damp environments, is a key asthma trigger. In fact, mold is harmful to everyone, regardless of whether they suffer from asthma or allergies. To root it out, look for both obvious and hidden sources of dampness and moisture. That leaky pipe under the kitchen sink is obvious, but you also need to wipe down the shower after use and keep the drip pans in the air conditioner, refrigerator, and dehumidifier clean and dry.

When a baby becomes part of a household, everything changes. You'll need to find a room for the baby, to decorate and furnish the room, and to childproof your home to the best of your ability. And, even if your child does not have any special needs, you'll also want to consider providing an environmentally-conscious atmosphere for baby as well as the rest of the family.

The greening of the American home has taken hold. It now receives much attention from the news media, as well as many architects, interior designers, manufacturers, and retailers, all of whom have jumped on the environmental bandwagon. While this is a positive development, be discriminating. Before you invest in green products, do some research or talk to experts you trust about which products are useful and which are not. There's a lot out there—and much of it is expensive. You could end up spending unnecessary money on trendy ideas or products that are not really helpful or effective.

keeping it green

What scientists know for certain is that tiny, still-developing immune, hormonal, and nervous systems are more susceptible than those of adults to the harmful effects of environmental pollutants. But as information emerges almost daily about the pollutants lurking in what were once considered safe products, parents can easily fall prey to panic and resist making any selections at all.

"The idea is not to alarm parents," says interior designer Patricia Gaylor, of Little Falls, New Jersey, who specializes in green design. "But it is essential to avoid any materials that contain harmful chemicals, from carpeting to bedding to toys."

Gaylor advises concerned parents to ask a lot of questions, even if they seem annoying, when purchasing nursery or toddler products. "If you don't get the answer you want, don't buy it. Continue to do your research until you're satisfied with what you find."

air fresheners

"One of the most important things to consider in the nursery is the quality of the air," says interior designer Patricia Gaylor. "Paint, glue, finishes on new furniture, and fabrics all emit VOCs (Volatile Organic Compounds) into the air and create a sort of toxic soup of chemicals," she says. "You want to eliminate anything that can irritate small lungs, so make sure you question every product that goes into the room."

Using only no-VOC paints is an important first step. They are readily available and don't cost significantly more than other types of paint. And as long as weather permits, opening windows daily to let in fresh air is another smart step.

ABOVE Green products of all kinds—furniture, fabrics, toys, and more—are now readily available, helping to protect babies and young children from environmental pollutants.

OPPOSITE Baby furniture made of wood without harmful chemicals may be a little more expensive, but keeping your baby safe is worth the investment.

Go Green

Avoid baby furniture made with formaldehyde or other chemicals. Look for solid-wood furniture with no-VOC finishes.

resource guide

associations

American Academy of Pediatrics (AAP)

141 Northwest Point Blvd.

Elk Grove Village, IL 60007-1098

847-434-4000

www.aap.org

National organization of pediatric health providers offering information and a referral service.

American Association of Poison Control Centers (AAPCC)

3201 New Mexico Ave., Ste. 330

Washington, DC 20016

202-362-7217

Emergencies: 800-222-1222

www.aapcc.org

National organization that provides listings of local poison-control centers.

American Sudden Infant Death Syndrome (SIDS) Institute

2480 Windy Hill Rd., Ste. 380

Marietta, GA 30067

800-232-7437

www.sids.org

Provides related information.

National Kitchen and Bath Association (NKBA)

687 Willow Grove St.

Hackettstown, NJ 07840

800-843-6522

www.nkba.org

A national trade organization for kitchen and bath design professionals; offers consumers product information and a referral service.

Better Sleep Council (BSC)

333 Commerce St.

Alexandria, VA 22314

703-683-8371

www.bettersleep.org

Provides related consumer information.

Consumer Product Safety Commission (CPSC)

800-638-2772

www.cpsc.gov

Federal regulatory agency offering information about products and safety recalls.

International Association for Child Safety (IACS)

P.O. Box 801

Summit, NJ 07902

888-677-4227

www.iaf.com

Nonprofit organization that offers safety advice and referrals to child-safety professionals.

The following list of manufacturers and associations is meant to be a general guide to additional industry and product-related sources. It is not intended as a listing of products and manufacturers represented by the photographs in this book.

Juvenile Products Manufacturers Association (JPMA)

15000 Commerce Pkwy., Ste. C

Mt. Laurel, NJ 08054

856-638-0420

www.jpma.org

Trade organization representing child-care products manufacturers.

National Safety Council (NSC)

1121 Spring Lake Dr.

Itasca, IL 60143

800-621-7619

www.nsc.org

Nonprofit public service organization.

Window Covering Safety Council

355 Lexington Ave., Ste. 1700

New York, NY 10017

800-506-4636

www.windowcoverings.org

Provides consumer information on window-cord safety.

manufacturers

American Standard

1 Centennial Plaza, P. O. Box 6820

Piscataway, NJ 08855-6820

www.americanstandard-us.com

Manufactures plumbing and tile products.

Baby's Dream Nursery Furniture

1-800-TEL-CRIB

www.babysdream.com

Manufactures infant furniture and room decor.

Blonder Home Accents

3950 Prospect Ave.

Cleveland, OH 44115

800-321-4070

www.blonderhome.com

Manufactures wallcoverings and fabrics.

CoCaLo, Inc.

2920 Red Hill Ave.

Costa Mesa, CA 92626

714-434-7200

www.cocalo.com

Manufactures infant bedding and room decor.

Delta Faucet Co.

55 E. 111th St.

P.O. Box 40980

Indianapolis, IN 46280

317-848-1812

www.deltafaucet.com

Manufactures a variety of faucets and finishes for the kitchen and bath.

Dream Baby

www.dreambaby.com.au

International manufacturer of child-safety products.

resource guide

Dutch Boy/Crayola

www.dutchboy.com

Manufactures paint, including the Crayola Kid's Room Paint Colors line.

Enabling Devices

385 Warburton Ave.

Hastings-on-Hudson, NY 10706

800-832-8697

www.enablingdevices.com

Manufactures products and toys for children with special needs.

Finn + Hattie

P.O. Box 539

Yarmouth, ME 04096

207-846-9166

www.finnandhattie.com

Manufactures juvenile furniture.

The First Years

One Kiddie Dr.

Boston, MA 02322

800-225-0382

www.thefirstyears.com

Manufactures baby bathtubs, gates, and monitors.

Forbo Flooring US

2 Maplewood Dr.

P.O. Box 667

Hazleton, PA 18201

866-Marmoleum

www.forbo.com

Manufactures eco-friendly Marmoleum floors.

Gund

1 Runyons Ln.

Edison, NJ 08817

www.gund.com

Manufactures plush toys.

Hunter-Douglas Window Fashions

2 Park Way

Upper Saddle River, NJ 07458

800-789-0331

www.hunterdouglas.com

Manufactures window treatments.

Infant Interiors

8 Freebody St., #1

Newport, RI 02840

401-842-0010

www.infantinteriors.com

Complete furnishings, bedding, lighting, and accessories for the nursery.

Kids II

1015 Windward Ridge Pkwy.

Alpharetta, GA 30005

770-751-0442

www.kidsii.com

Distributes children's safety products and toys.

Kohler

444 Highland Dr.

Kohler, WI 53044

800-456-4537

www.kohlerco.com

Manufactures kitchen and bath sinks, faucets, and related accessories.

Lambs & Ivy

5978 Bowcroft St.

Los Angeles, CA 90016

800-345-2626

www.lambsandivy.com

Manufactures juvenile bedding and accessories.

Merillat Industries

5353 W. U.S. 223

P.O. Box 1946

Adrian, MI 49221

800-575-8763

www.merillat.com

Manufactures kitchen and bath cabinetry.

Motif Designs

20 Jones St.

New Rochelle, NY 10802

www.motif-designs.com

Manufactures fabrics and wallcoverings.

Prince Lionheart, Inc.,

2421 S. Westgate Rd.

Santa Maria, CA 93455

805-922-2250

www.princelionheart.com

Manufactures diaper disposal systems, baby-wipe warmers, and more.

Seabrook Wallcoverings

1325 Farmville Rd.

Memphis, TN 38122

800-238-9152

www.seabrookwallpaper.com

Manufactures wallcoverings.

Sherwin Williams

www.sherwinwilliams.com

Manufactures paint.

Stencil Ease

P.O. Box 1127

Old Saybrook, CT 06475

800-334-1776

www.stencilease.com

Manufactures decorative wall stencils, tools, and supplies.

The Well-Appointed House

19 E. 65th St., Ste. 7B

New York, NY

888-935-5277

www.wellappointedhouse.com

Sells juvenile furnishings nationwide.

resource guide

Wilsonart International

P.O. Box 6110

Temple, TX 76503-6110

800-433-3222

www.wilsonart.com

Manufactures solid-surfacing material, plastic laminate, and adhesive for floors, cabinets, and countertops.

York Wallcoverings

700 Linden Ave.

York, PA 17404

717-846-4456

www.yorkwall.com

Manufactures wallcoverings and borders.

architects & designers

Little Crown Interiors/Rugrat Habitats

3303 Harbor Blvd., Ste. C4

Costa Mesa, CA 92626

714-253-2426

www.rugrat-habitat.com

www.littlecrowninteriors.com

Leslie Saul & Associates Architecture & Interiors

1972 Massachusetts Ave.

Cambridge, MA 02140

617-234-5300, ext. 16

Patricia Gaylor Interior Design

265 Long Hill Rd.

Little Falls, NJ 07424

201-396-9297

www.PatriciaGaylor.com

Vivavi Green Furniture and Furnishings

Showroom: The Riverhouse

Apt. 8D

2 River Terr.

New York, NY 10282

866-848-2840

www.vivavi.com

Many thanks to the following for their invaluable assistance in the production of this book:

Blik

www.whatisblik.com

866-262-2545

Designs self-adhesive decorative wall graphics.

Boodalee

888-864-7819

www.boodalee.com

Designs children's bedding and accessories with a modern aesthetic.

DwellStudio

155 Sixth Ave. 7th Fl.

New York, NY 10013

212-219-9343

www.dwellshop.com

Designer of contemporary bedding, pillows, and home accessories for infants, children, and adults.

Fawn & Forest

800-385-0703

www.fawnandforest.com

Online retailer of organic and eco-friendly children's furniture, bedding, toys, and clothing.

The Land of Nod

800-933-9904

www.landofnod.com

Sells juvenile furniture, cribs, bedding, and room decor.

Oopsy Daisy, Fine Art for Kids

619-640-6649

www.oopsydaisy.com

Sells wall art, lighting, and accessories for nurseries and children's rooms.

Posh Tots

866-POSHTOT (866-767-4868)

www.poshtots.com

Sells infant's and children's luxury furniture, bedding, and room decor.

Sparkability

www.sparkability.net

Features modern-design children's furnishings, toys, and accessories.

glossary

Accessible Designs: Any design that accommodates persons with physical disabilities.

Acrylic Paint: A water-soluble paint with a plastic polymer (acrylic) binder.

Adaptable Designs: Any design that can be easily adjusted to accommodate a person with disabilities.

Analogous Scheme: See Harmonious Color Scheme.

Armoire: A large, often ornate, cupboard or wardrobe that is used for storage.

Asymmetry: As a decorating concept, the balance between different-size objects, parts, or forms as the result of placement. An example of an asymmetrical arrangement is that of a window treatment consisting of a scarf valance that is draped over a curtain rod in such a way that the tail on one end is longer than the tail on the other end.

Audio and Video Monitor: A high-tech version of a baby monitor that lets you see as well as hear your baby when you are not in the same room. Some versions combine a digital camera with a computer so that you can watch your baby through an Internet connection when you are away from home.

Baby Monitor: An electric or battery-powered device that consists of a transmitter and a receiver, which enables you to hear what is happening in the nursery when you are out of the room. Some monitors have walkie-talkie features, allowing you to talk to the baby from another location in and around the house.

Balance: As a decorating concept, the equilibrium among the objects or forms in a room that appears natural and comfortable to the eye. For example, two pictures of relatively equal size and weight balance each other and look pleasing as a pair on a wall. Balance can also apply to color or other aspects of the elements in a room.

Bassinet: A newborn baby's bed that is shaped like a basket with a hood at one end. A bassinet is lightweight and traditionally made of wicker, although it can also be made of plastic. A bassinet has a stand with wheels or castors that lock for safety.

Built-in: Any element, such as a bookcase or cabinetry, that is built into a wall or an existing frame.

Bumpers: Padded cushions that are attached to the side rails of a crib.

Case Goods: Furniture used for storage, including cabinets, dressers, and desks.

Chaise Longue: A chair with back support and a seat long enough for outstretched legs.

Changing Table: A stand-alone padded table that is used for changing the baby. Some changing tables are dressers with an attached or portable raised deck that is equipped with a pad. The deck can be removed when a changing table is no longer needed.

Clearance: The amount of space between two fixtures, the centerlines of two fixtures, or a fixture and an obstacle, such as a wall. Clearances may be mandated by codes.

Code: A locally or nationally enforced mandate regarding structural design, materials, plumbing, or electrical systems that state what you can or cannot do when you build or remodel. Codes are intended to protect standards of health, safety, and land use.

Color Scheme: A group of colors used together to create visual harmony in a space.

Color Wheel: A diagram showing the range and relationships of pigment and dye colors. Three equidistant wedge-shaped slices are the primary colors; in between are the secondary and tertiary colors into which the primaries combine. Though represented as discrete slices, the hues form a continuum.

Complementary Colors: Hues directly opposite each other on the color wheel. As the strongest contrasts, complementary colors tend to intensify each other. A color can be grayed by mixing it with its complement.

Contemporary: Any modern design (after 1920) that does not contain or refer to traditional elements of the past.

Convertible Crib: A crib that converts to a junior bed or a twin- or full-size bed.

Contrast: The art of assembling colors with different values and intensities and in different proportions to create a dynamic scheme.

Cradle: An infant's bed that is made of wood and has rockers.

Crib Railings: The usually slatted enclosures on both sides of a crib that can be adjusted to a high or low position. Slats should be spaced no more than 2⅜ inches apart to prevent accidents.

Daybed: A bed made up to appear as a sofa. It usually has a frame that consists of a headboard, a footboard, and a sideboard along the back.

Dehumidifier: A device that reduces the amount of moisture in the air without cooling it.

Floor Plan: A layout of a room that has been drawn to scale.

Focal Point: The dominant element in a room or design, usually the first to catch your eye.

Genuine Wood Furniture: A label on a piece of furniture indicating that all of the exposed parts are made of a veneer (of a specified wood) over hardwood or plywood.

Hardware: Wood, plastic, or metal-plated trim found on the exterior of furniture, such as knobs, handles, locks, hinges, and decorative trim.

Harmony: As a decorating concept, harmony is the continuity between the different elements of a room. For example, sleek unfettered designs are harmonious with contemporary architecture.

Harmonious Color Scheme: Also called analogous, a combination focused on neighboring hues on the color wheel. The shared underlying color generally gives such schemes a coherent flow.

Hue: Specific points on the pure, clear range of the color wheel. Also, another term for color.

Incandescent Lamp: A bulb that contains a conductive filament through which current flows. The current reacts with an inert gas inside the bulb, which makes the filament glow.

Indirect Lighting: A subdued type of lighting that is not head-on, but reflected against another surface, such as a ceiling.

glossary

Innerspring Mattress: A mattress with coil springs. The higher the coil count, the more support it provides. The minimum coil count for a crib mattress is 150. Twin-size mattresses should have at least 200 coils.

Junior Bed: A transitional bed for a toddler. A junior bed, also known as a "youth bed," uses a crib-size mattress. Some cribs convert to a junior bed.

Laminate: One or more thin layers of melamine or other durable plastic that is bonded to a fabric or a material. It may be used on furniture, countertops, and floors.

Latex Paint: A water-soluble, quick-drying paint that contains either acrylic or vinyl resins or a combination of the two. High-quality latex paints contain 100 percent acrylic resin.

Man-Made Materials: A furniture label that refers to plastic-laminate panels that are printed to look like wood. The furniture may also include plastic that has been molded to look like wood carving or trim.

Mobile: A mechanical wheel with suspended shapes that hangs above the crib or over the changing table. A wind-up mechanism or battery-operated device sets the mobile in motion and activates optional sound features.

Modular Furniture: Units of a standard size, such as chests and dressers, that are not built-in and can be used separately or fitted together in a number of arrangements.

Molding: An architectural band that can either trim a line where materials join or create a linear decoration at the top of a cabinet or on the wall. It is typically made of wood, but metal, plaster, or polymer (plastic) is also used.

Natural Fibers: Any fibers or fabrics that are not manmade. These include cotton, linen, wool, and silk.

Orientation: The placement of any object or space, such as a window, door, or room, and its relationship to the points on a compass.

Overall: A term for a pattern on fabric or wallcovering that is even and overall or random. An overall pattern is most commonly used on curtains.

Palette: See Color Scheme.

Panel: A flat, rectangular piece of material that forms part of a wall, door, or cabinet. Typically made of wood, it is usually framed by a border and either raised or recessed.

Parquet: Inlaid woodwork arranged to form a geometric pattern on a floor. It consists of small blocks of hardwood, which are often stained in contrasting colors.

Pattern Matching: To align a repeating pattern when joining together two pieces of fabric or wallpaper.

Pocket Door: A door that slides into the wall when it is open.

Polyurethane: A tough, hard-wearing coating made of synthetic resins. It serves as a good top coat or finish and can be applied over most types of painted- or stained-wood surfaces, such as furniture or floors. Nonyellowing polyester produces a clear finish.

Primary Color: Red, blue, or yellow, which can't be produced in pigments by mixing other colors. Primaries plus black and white, in turn, combine to make all the other hues.

Primer: A coating that prepares surfaces for painting by making them more uniform in texture and giving them "tooth."

Proportion: The relationship of parts or objects to one another based on size. For example, the size of a baby's shoes is in proportion to the size of her feet.

Ready-Made: A term used to describe something that has been mass-produced in standard sizes, such as curtains or slipcovers.

Rhythm: A decorating concept that refers to any form of repetition that coordinates visual elements. For example, repeated patterns, colors, or themes.

Sample: A small piece or cutting from a roll of wallcovering or a bolt of fabric that is used to test at home or as a reference for coordinating colors and prints.

Sample Board: A small, typically foam-cored board that is used to hold and try out swatches, samples, and color chips. The various samples should be displayed on the board in proportion to how they would appear in the room for an accurate evaluation of the projected overall design.

Safety Gate: A barrier that can be mounted to walls or installed in door and window frames to keep a baby from wandering or from injury.

Scale: The size of something as it relates to the size of everything else. For example, babies are small, adults are large.

Sealer: A coating that is applied to porous surfaces before painting in order to form a durable, nonabsorbent barrier between the surface and the paint. A sealer facilitates a smooth and even finish.

Secondary Color: A mix of two primaries. The secondary colors are orange, green, and purple.

Sensor Pad: A feature of some baby monitors. A sensor pad is a thin, almost flat transmitter that fits under the crib mattress. It detects the slightest movements of a baby, sounds an alarm, and signals the receiver if the infant is absolutely motionless for more than 20 seconds.

Shade: A color to which black or gray has been added to make it darker.

Sheen: The quality of paint that reflects light when it is dry. It can range from mat-

ted (completely nonreflective) to high gloss (very shiny).

Stencil: A cut-out pattern.

Solid Wood: A furniture label indicating that the exposed surfaces are made of wood without any veneer or plywood.

Sudden Infant Death Syndrome (SIDS): The sudden death of a baby under 1 year old.

Swatch: A cutting or sample of a piece of fabric.

Symmetry: The exact arrangement of objects, parts, or forms on both sides of an imagined or real center line. An example of a symmetrical arrangement is that of a window treatment consisting of a scarf valance that is draped over a curtain rod in such a way that the tails on either side are the same length.

Synthetic Fibers: Man-made alternatives to natural fibers. Examples include polyester, nylon, rayon, and acetate.

Stenciling: Creating an image or a motif, often in a repeated pattern, by painting on a cutout pattern.

Ticking: A strong, closely woven cotton that usually has stripes.

Tint: A color to which white or light gray has been added to make it lighter.

Tone: The degree of lightness or darkness of a color. A color to which gray has been added to change its value.

Trompe L'oeil: Literally meaning "fool the eye;" a painted mural in which realistic images and the illusion three-dimensional space are created. Also, a painted surface that convincingly mimics reality.

Youth Bed: See Junior Bed.

Value: In relation to a scale of grays ranging from black to white, the lightness (tints) or darkness (shades) of a color.

Veneer: High-quality wood that is cut into very thin sheets for use as a surface material—on a piece of furniture, for example.

Wainscoting: Traditionally, paneling or woodwork that covers the lower third of the wall.

Wash: A thinned-out latex or acrylic paint.

Welt: A cord, often covered with fabric, that is used to trim cushions or slipcovers.

Wood: A furniture label that indicates that none of the parts of the furniture are made of plastic, metal, or anything other than wood.

index

index

photo credits

page 1: courtesy of DwellStudio pages 3–4: courtesy of PoshTots.com pages 6–7: *left* Mark Lohman, design: Rugrat Habitat/Little Crown Interiors; *top right* courtesy of Fawn and Forest; *bottom right* courtesy of PoshTots.com pages 8–9: courtesy of York Wallcoverings pages 10–11: *all* courtesy of Fawn and Forest page 12: Bob Greenspan, stylist: Susan Andrews page 13: *left* courtesy of York Wallcoverings *right* Mark Samu/CH pages 14–15: courtesy of PoshTots.com pages 16–17: *left* courtesy of Seabrook Wallcoverings; *right* courtesy of York Wallcoverings page 18: courtesy of Blonder Home page 19: Mark Samu/CH pages 20–21: Eric Roth page 22: *top* Mark Samu/CH; *bottom* courtesy of Stencil Ease page 23: courtesy of Thibaut page 24: Mark Samu/CH page 25: courtesy of Posh-Tots.com pages 26: courtesy of CoCaLo Couture, design: Chad Gorenhuf-Burke Design page 27: *top left* courtesy of CoCaLo Couture, design: Chad Gorenhuf-Burke Design; *top right* courtesy of York Wallcoverings; *bottom* courtesy of Blonder Home page 28: *all* Mark Samu/CH page 29: *top* Eric Roth; *bottom* courtesy of Hunter Douglas page 30: courtesy of Posh-Tots.com page 31: *all* Mark Samu/CH; *bottom* design: Ken Kelly pages 32–33: Karyn R. Millet, design: Bonesteel Trout Hall page 34: Mark Samu, design: Pascucci/Delisle Design page 35: Eric Roth pages 36–37: *left* courtesy of Sparkability; *right* courtesy of Fawn and Forest page 38: *top* courtesy of Blik; *bottom* courtesy of York Wallcoverings page 40: courtesy of Gund page 41: courtesy of Blonder Home page 42: Mark Samu/CH page 43: *top* courtesy of York Wallcoverings; *bottom* Mark Samu/CH pages 44–45: *top left* & *bottom* courtesy of Fawn and Forest; *left* courtesy of Picture Perfect

Design pages 46–47: *all* courtesy of York Wallcoverings page 48: courtesy of PoshTots.com page 49: *left* courtesy of Sparkability; *right* courtesy of PoshTots.com page 50: *top* Eric Roth; *bottom* courtesy of Blik page 51: courtesy of York Wallcoverings pages 52–53: *all* courtesy of Blonder Home pages 54–55: *left* courtesy of Lambs & Ivy; *right* Eric Roth pages 56–57: *all* Bob Greenspan, stylist: Susan Andrews pages 58–59: Mark Lohman, design: Rugrat Habitat/Little Crown Interiors page 60: Mark Samu/CH page 61: *top* & *bottom left* Mark Lohman, design: Sue McKeehan; *bottom right* Mark Samu, design: Correia Design pages 62–63: Olson Photographic, LLC, design: Infant Interiors pages 64–65: *left* Olson Photographic, LLC, design: Infant Interiors; *right* Mark Samu/CH pages 66–67: Olson Photographic, LLC, design: Infant Interiors page 68: Tria Giovan Photography page 69: Olson Photographic, LLC, design: Infant Interiors page 70: *top* Olson Photographic, LLC, design: Infant Interiors; *bottom* courtesy of Fawn and Forest page 71: *top* Mark Samu/CH; *bottom* Tria Giovan Photography pages 72–73: *top left* courtesy of Fawn and Forest; *top* & *bottom right* Mark Lohman, design: Rugrat Habitat/Little Crown Interiors; *bottom left* Mark Samu page 74: *top* design by Lyn Peterson for Motif Designs; *bottom* Olson Photographic, LLC page 75: courtesy of York Wallcoverings page 76: Mark Samu/CH page 77: courtesy of York Wallcoverings pages 78–79: Mark Lohman, design: Rugrat Habitat/Little Crown Interiors pages 80–81: *top left* & *right* Mark Lohman, design: Rugrat Habitat/Little Crown Interiors; *bottom* courtesy of Dutch Boy/Crayola pages 82–83: *left* courtesy of Posh-Tots.com; center courtesy of Dutch

Boy/Crayola; *right* courtesy of Finn + Hattie page 84: courtesy of Fawn and Forest page 85: courtesy of Boodalee page 86: *top* & *bottom* Tony Glammarino/Giammarino & Dworkin, *top* design: Karen Adams, *bottom* painter: Beth Scherr page 87: *top* courtesy of York Wallcoverings; *bottom all* courtesy of Blonder Home page 88: *all* courtesy of Blonder Home pages 89–90: *all* courtesy of York Wallcoverings page 91: Mark Lohman pages 92–93: Karyn R. Millet, design: Elizabeth Dinkel Design Associates pages 94–95: *left* Eric Roth; center Olson Photographic, LLC, design: Infant Interiors; *right* courtesy of York Wallcoverings page 96: *top* Tony Giammarino/Giammarino & Dworkin, design: Karen Adams; *bottom* Minh + Wass page 97: courtesy of Blonder Home page 98: *top* Tony Giammarino/Giammarino & Dworkin, design: Karen Adams; *bottom* courtesy of Dutch Boy/Crayola page 99: Olson Photography, LLC, design: Infant Interiors pages 100–101: *left* courtesy of Forbo Flooring Systems, collection: Marmoleum Click; *right* courtesy of DwellStudio page 102: Mark Lohman, design: Rugrat Habitat/Little Crown Interiors page 103: courtesy of Armstrong page 104: Karyn R. Millet, design: Bonesteel Trout Hall page 105: *top* courtesy of PoshTots.com; *bottom* courtesy of DwellStudio page 106: Mark Lohman, design: Rugrat Habitat/Little Crown Interiors page 107: Tony Giammarino/Giammarino & Dworkin, design: Karen Adams pages 108–109: courtesy of DwellStudio pages 110–111: *left* Mark Samu, design: Pascucci/Delisle Design; *right* Karyn R. Millet pages 112–113: *left* courtesy of The Well Appointed House; *top right* courtesy of PoshTots.com; *bottom right* Eric Roth pages 114–115: *top left* courtesy of

PoshTots.com; *bottom left* courtesy of Land of Nod; center Olson Photography, LLC, design: Infant Interiors; *right* courtesy of Fawn and Forest **pages 116–117:** *all* Mark Lohman, *left* design: Andy Marcus, *right* design: Rugrat Habitat/Little Crown Interiors **page 118:** *top* Kevin cFeely/RedCover.com; *bottom* Karyn R. Millet, design: Elizabeth Dinkel Design Associates **page 119:** courtesy of DwellStudio **page 120:** *all* courtesy of Land of Nod **page 121:** *top* courtesy of DwellStudio; *bottom* Mark Lohman, design: Rugrat Habitat/Little Crown Interiors **page 122:** *top* courtesy of Land of Nod; *bottom* Mark Lohman, design: Rugrat Habitat/Little Crown Interiors **page 123:** *top* Mark Lohman, design: Rugrat Habitat/Little Crown Interiors; *bottom* courtesy of Land of Nod **pages 124–125:** *top left* Mark Lohman, design: Rugrat Habitat/Little Crown Interiors; *top right* courtesy of Fawn and Forest; *bottom right* Mark Lohman, design: Rugrat Habitat/Little Crown Interiors; *bottom left* courtesy of Blonder Home **page 126:** *top* Mark Lohman, design: Rugrat Habitat/Little Crown Interiors; *bottom* courtesy of Fawn and Forest **page 127:** Mark Lohman, design: Rugrat Habitat/Little Crown Interiors **pages 128–129:** *all* Mark Lohman, design: Rugrat Habitat/Little Crown Interiors **page 130:** *top* Mark Lohman, design: Rugrat Habitat/Little Crown Interiors; *bottom* courtesy of PoshTots.com **page 131:** Mark Lohman, design: Rugrat Habitat/Little Crown Interiors **pages 132–133:** *top left* courtesy of PoshTots.com; *top right* Mark Lohman, design: Rugrat Habitat/Little Crown Interiors; *bottom right* courtesy of Fawn and Forest; center Mark Lohman, design: Rugrat Habitat/Little Crown Interiors; *bottom left* courtesy of PoshTots.com **page**

134: Mark Lohman, design: Rugrat Habitat/Little Crown Interiors **page 135:** *top* Winfried Heinze/Red-Cover.com, architect: Studio Azzurro; *bottom* Mark Lohman, design: Rugrat Habitat/Little Crown Interiors **pages 136–137:** Jessie Walker **page 138:** *top left* courtesy of Oopsy Daisy; *top right* courtesy of PoshTots.com; *bottom* courtesy of York Wallcoverings **page 139:** Bob Greenspan, stylist: Susan Andrews **pages 140–141:** courtesy of York Wallcoverings **page 142:** *top* courtesy of York Wallcoverings; *bottom* courtesy of PoshTots.com **page 142:** courtesy of PoshTots.com **page 144:** *top* courtesy of Blue Mountain Wallcoverings; *bottom* courtesy of Posh-Tots.com **page 145:** *top* courtesy of Dutch Boy/Crayola; *bottom all* courtesy of PoshTots.com **page 146:** Minh+Wass **page 147:** Mark Lohman, design: Sue McKeehan **pages 148–149:** *top left* Eric Roth; *top* center courtesy of Boodalee; *top right* Olson Photography, LLC, design: Infant Interiors; *bottom right* courtesy of York Wallcoverings; *bottom left* courtesy of PoshTots.com **page 150:** courtesy of Blonder Home **page 151:** *top left* courtesy of Oopsy Daisy; *top right* Tony Giammarino/Giammarino & Dworkin, design: Karen Adams; center courtesy of PoshTots.com; *bottom* courtesy of Oopsy Daisy **page 152:** courtesy of Oopsy Daisy **page 153:** *top left* Red-Cover.com; *top right* Minh+Wass; *bottom* courtesy of Fawn and Forest **page 154:** *top* courtesy of IKEA; *bottom* Mark Lohman, design: Rugrat Habitat/Little Crown Interiors **page 155:** *top* courtesy of Forbo Flooring Systems; *bottom* Mark Lohman, design: Rugrat Habitat/Little Crown Interiors **page 156:** *top* Minh+Wass; *bottom* Mark Lohman, design: Rugrat Habitat/Little Crown Interiors

page 157: courtesy of PoshTots.com **page 158:** *left* courtesy of Dutch Boy/Cray-ola; *top right* courtesy of Finn + Hattie; *bottom right* Mark Lohman, design: Rugrat Habitat/Little Crown Interiors **pages 159–161:** *all* courtesy of York Wallcoverings **pages 162–163:** *top left* & *right* Mark Lohman, design: Rugrat Habitat/Little Crown Interiors; *bottom left* & *right* courtesy of Dutch Boy/ Crayola **pages 164–165:** courtesy of DwellStudio **page 166:** courtesy of Blonder Home **page 168:** *top* courtesy of PoshTots.com; *bottom* courtesy of Kids II **page 169:** courtesy of KooKoo Bear Kids **pages 170–171:** *top left* courtesy of Forever Mine; *right* courtesy of Dutch Boy/Crayola; *bottom left* courtesy of Boodalee **page 172:** courtesy of PoshTots.com **page 173:** Olson Photographic, LLC **page 174:** *top* courtesy of Fawn and Forest; *bottom* courtesy of Dream Baby **page 175:** Trine Thorsen/RedCover.com **pages 176–177:** *left* courtesy of York Wallcoverings; *top right* courtesy of Sparkability; *bottom right* courtesy of The First Years **page 178:** *all* courtesy of Merillat **page 179:** davidduncanlivingston.com **pages 180–181:** Nina Assam/Red-Cover.com **pages 182–183:** *left* courtesy of Sparkability; *right* courtesy of Dutch Boy/Crayola **pages 184–185:** *left* Lucinda Symons/Red Cover.com; *right* Sasfi Hope-Ross/RedCover.com **page 187:** courtesy of PoshTots.com **page 188:** courtesy of DwellStudio **page 189:** *top* courtesy of CoCaLo Couture, design: Chad Gorenhuf-Burke Design; *bottom* courtesy of PoshTots.com **page 190:** courtesy of Fawn and Forest **page 191:** courtesy of PoshTots.com **page 197:** Olson Photographic, LLC, design: Infant Interiors **page 198:** courtesy of Land of Nod **page 204:** courtesy of Blonder Home

If you like

Design Ideas for Baby Rooms,

take a look at these and other books in the

Design Ideas Series

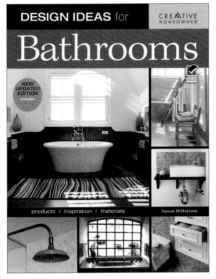

Design Ideas for Bathrooms
Design inspiration for creating a new and
improved bathroom. Over 500 photos.
224 pp.; 8½" x 10⅞"
BOOK #279261
REVISED AND EXPANDED

Design Ideas for Basements
Design solutions for putting your basement space to good use. Over 300 color
photos. 208 pp.; 8½" x 10⅞"
BOOK #279424

Design Ideas for Kitchens
Design inspiration and new product ideas
for creating a dream kitchen. Over 500
photos. 224 pp.; 8½" x 10⅞"
BOOK #279412
REVISED AND EXPANDED

Design Ideas for Decks & Patios
The latest design trends for fabulous
backyard living spaces. Over 350 photos.
224 pp.; 8½" x 10⅞"
BOOK #279534

Design Ideas for Home Decorating
Design solutions for every room, on every
budget. Over 500 photos.
320 pp.; 8½" x 10⅞"
BOOK #279323

Design Ideas for Home Landscaping
Inspiring ideas to achieve stunning
effects with your landscape. Over 350
photos. 240 pp; 8½" x 10⅞"
BOOK #274154

For more information and to order direct, go to **www.creativehomeowner.com**